SCHOLASTIC

Health & Wellbeing

- Links to *Every Child Matters* and *SEAL*
- CD-ROM includes interactive activities
- Differentiated photocopiables provided
- Easy-to-use interactive whiteboard tools

Angie Cooper
and Julia Stanton

AGES 9-11

Terms and conditions

IMPORTANT – PERMITTED USE AND WARNINGS – READ CAREFULLY BEFORE USING

Licence

Copyright in the software contained in this CD-ROM and in its accompanying material belongs to Scholastic Limited. All rights reserved. © 2008 Scholastic Ltd.

Save for these purposes, or as expressly authorised in the accompanying materials, the software may not be copied, reproduced, used, sold, licensed, transferred, exchanged, hired, or exported in whole or in part or in any manner or form without the prior written consent of Scholastic Ltd. Any such unauthorised use or activities are prohibited and may give rise to civil liabilities and criminal prosecutions.

The material contained on this CD-ROM may only be used in the context for which it was intended in *Health & Wellbeing*, and is for use only in the school which has purchased the book and CD-ROM, or by the teacher who has purchased the book and CD-ROM. Permission to download images is given for purchasers only and not for users from any lending service. Any further use of the material contravenes Scholastic Ltd's copyright and that of other rights' holders.

This CD-ROM has been tested for viruses at all stages of its production. However, we recommend that you run virus-checking software on your computer systems at all times. Scholastic Ltd cannot accept any responsibility for any loss, disruption or damage to your data or your computer system that may occur as a result of using either the CD-ROM or the data held on it.

Credits

Authors
Angie Cooper & Julia Stanton

Project Manager
Julia Stanton

Editor
Sara Wiegand

Cover Designer
Allison Parry

Series Designer
Anna Oliwa

Designer
Christina Newman (Black Dog Design)

Illustrations
Celia Hart, Beverly Curl

CD-ROM programming and illustration
e-s-p ltd 2008

Acknowledgements

Material from the National Curriculum © Crown copyright.

Every effort has been made to trace copyright holders for the works reproduced in this book, and the publishers apologise for any inadvertent omissions.

Minimum specification:
- PC with CD-ROM drive: Windows 98 or higher
- Processor: Pentium 2 (or equivalent) 1000 MHz
- RAM: 512 Mb
- Graphics card and colour monitor capable of displaying 24- bit colour graphics at a resolution of at least 1024x768 pixels.

- Mac with CD-ROM drive: OS X and above
- Processor: G3 1000 MHz
- RAM: 512 Mb
- Graphics card and colour monitor capable of displaying 24- bit colour graphics at a resolution of at least 1024x768 pixels.

Published by Scholastic Ltd
Villiers House
Clarendon Avenue
Leamington Spa
Warks. CV32 5PR
www.scholastic.co.uk

Designed using Adobe InDesign

Printed by Bell and Bain Ltd

123456789   8901234567

Text © 2008 Angie Cooper & Julia Stanton

© 2008 Scholastic Ltd

British Library Cataloguing-in-Publication Data
A catalogue record for this book is available from the British Library.

ISBN 978-1407-10023-4

The rights of Angie Cooper and Julia Stanton as the authors of this work have been asserted by them in accordance with the Copyright, Designs and Patents Act 1988.

All rights reserved. This book is sold subject to the condition that it shall not, by way of trade or otherwise, be lent, hired out or otherwise circulated without the publisher's prior consent in any form of binding or cover other than that in which it is published and without a similar condition, including this condition, being imposed upon the subsequent purchaser.

No part of this publication may be reproduced, stored in a retrieval system, or transmitted, in any form or by any means, electronic, mechanical, photocopying, recording or otherwise, other than for the purposes described in the lessons in this book, without the prior permission of the publisher. This book remains copyright, although permission is granted to copy pages where indicated for classroom distribution and use only in the school which has purchased the book, or by the teacher who has purchased the book, and in accordance with the CLA licensing agreement. Photocopying permission is given only for purchasers and not for borrowers of books from any lending service.

Due to the nature of the web, the publisher cannot guarantee the content or links of any of the websites referred to in this book. It is the responsibility of the reader to assess the suitability of websites. Ensure you read and abide by the terms and conditions of websites when you use material from website links.

Contents

Introduction — 7
About the book — 7
PSHE in the classroom — 9
About the series — 11
How to use the CD-ROM — 14

Unit 1 Discovering myself — 16
Unit planner — 16
Let's talk — 18
Activities 1–12 — 19
Photocopiable pages — 25
Self-evaluation sheet — 28

Unit 2 Good days and bad days — 29
Unit planner — 29
Let's talk — 31
Activities 1–12 — 32
Photocopiable pages — 38
Self-evaluation sheet — 41

Unit 3 A healthy lifestyle — 42
Unit planner — 42
Let's talk — 44
Activities 1–12 — 45
Photocopiable pages — 51
Self-evaluation sheet — 54

Unit 4 Am I safe? — 55
Unit planner — 55
Let's talk — 57
Activities 1–12 — 58
Photocopiable pages — 64
Self-evaluation sheet — 67

Unit 5 Relationships — 68
Unit planner — 68
Let's talk — 70
Activities 1–12 — 71
Photocopiable pages — 77
Self-evaluation sheet — 80

Unit 6 My community and environment — 81
Unit planner — 81
Let's talk — 83
Activities 1–12 — 84
Photocopiable pages — 90
Self-evaluation sheet — 93

CD-ROM contents

Unit 1 Discovering myself
Interactive activities:
Personal qualities quiz
Body image advice
Why didn't you do your homework?
Photocopiables:
My autobiographical poem (C)
My autobiographical poem (S)
My autobiographical poem (E)
Little eyes upon you (C)
Little eyes upon you (S)
Little eyes upon you (E)
Responsible behaviour (C)
Responsible behaviour (S)
That's irresponsible! (E)
Self-evaluation: All about me
Photos:
Children and young people
Templates, cards and illustrations:
Negative thoughts
Family traits
'Eat Joosy Frooty Choos'
How to say 'No'
Peer pressure scenarios
Little Eyes Upon You
How to be responsible
Sentence stems
Children's booklet:
Self-evaluation: Discovering myself

Unit 2 Good days and bad days
Interactive activities:
What would a trustworthy person do?
Choose your words carefully
Consequences of anger
Photocopiables:
Name that feeling (C)
Name that feeling (S)
Name that feeling (E)

Photocopiables
C = Core
S = Support
E = Extension

CD-ROM contents

What can I say? (C)
What can I say? (S)
What can I say? (E)
Courage profile (C)
Courage profile (S)
Courage profile (E)
Self-evaluation: Good days and bad days
Photos:
Body language
Templates, cards and illustrations:
Mr Nobody
Memory chart
How stressful is that?
Shooting star
What is courage?
Showing we care
What would you say?
Great expectations
Children's booklet:
My feelings

Unit 3 A healthy lifestyle
Interactive activities:
Healthy lifestyle quiz
How do they rank?
Saying 'yes' or 'no'
Photocopiables:
Staying healthy (C)
Staying healthy (S)
Staying healthy (E)
Nutrition labels (C)
Nutrition labels (S)
Nutrition labels (E)
Leisure time (C)
Leisure time (S)
Leisure time (E)
Self-evaluation: Healthy living and me
Photos:
Different sports
Leisure time

CD-ROM contents

Templates, cards and illustrations:
Food diary
Healthy food pyramid
Food and drink advertising
Why exercise?
All different
Personal health
Positive and negative responses
Stress metre
More responsibilities
In the hot seat
Children's booklet:
My healthy lifestyle

Unit 4 Am I safe?
Interactive activities:
What would a safe person do?
Sports safety equipment
Choose your words
Photocopiables:
Risks at home (C)
Risks at home (S)
Risks at home (E)
Is it safe? (C)
Is it safe? (S)
Is it safe? (E)
Danger! (C)
Danger! (S)
Danger! (E)
Self-evaluation: Keeping safe
Photos:
Road safety signs
Natural disasters
Templates, cards and illustrations:
Safety web
Online chat
Still life
If, then
Constructing an advertisement
Be cautious

Natural disasters
Safety responsibilities
Safety at school
Children's booklet:
Am I safe?

Unit 5 Relationships
Interactive activities:
Aspects of bullying
How to be fair 1
How to be fair 2
Respect
Photocopiables:
How to be a good friend (C)
How to be a good friend (S)
How to be a good friend (E)
All change (C)
All change (S)
All change (E)
Can we talk? (C)
Can we talk? (S)
Can we talk? (E)
Self-evaluation: Relationships
Photos:
Gender roles
Templates, cards and illustrations:
How to beat prejudice
Crabby Old Woman
The gang rules!
What bullies do
How to be respectful
Girls and boys
I need to talk
Make the right choice
Children's booklet:
Relationships

Unit 6 My community and environment

Interactive activities:
Needs and wants
The law
Breaking the law

Photocopiables:
Needs and wants – a different perspective (C)
Needs and wants – a different perspective (S)
Needs and wants – a different perspective (E)
Survey of facilities for disabled people
Cheating (C)
Cheating (S)
Cheating (E)
Self-evaluation: My community and environment

Photos:
Necessity or luxury

Templates, cards and illustrations:
Different children
Have your say
Courtroom drama
Vandalism
Do's and don'ts
Rights of the child
Who does what?
Issue analysis
My view
Making a positive contribution
Rights and responsibilities
Arguments
Reflection

Children's booklet:
My community and environment

Introduction

About the book

This book is divided into six units (listed below) which have specific links to PSHE guidelines, *Every Child Matters* objectives and the SEAL guidance.
- Discovering myself
- Good days and bad days
- A healthy lifestyle
- Am I safe?
- Relationships
- My community and environment

Each of the units contains the following elements, some of which are in the book while others are found on the CD-ROM.

- Unit planner – A framework of reference and information for teachers.

- Let's Talk – Circle time questions to introduce the unit concepts and stimulate 'thinking' about the topic.

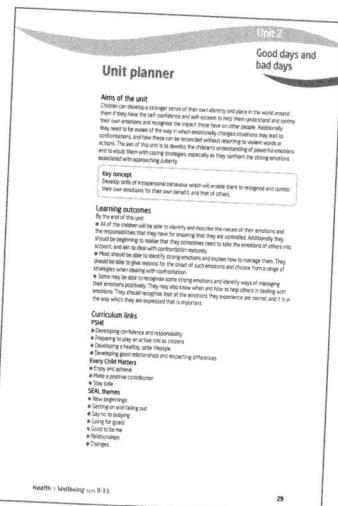

- Twelve activities for children, concluding with two 'reflection' activities. All other resources are cross-referred from the activities.

- Photocopiables – Three per unit, all of which are available as pdfs on the CD-ROM with differentiated photocopiables.

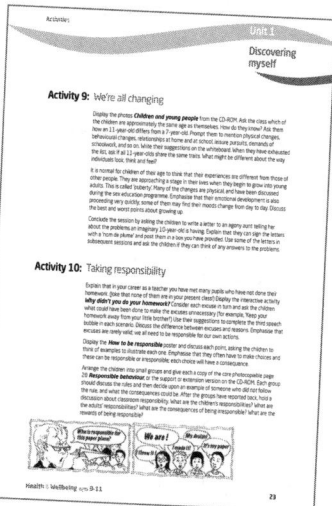

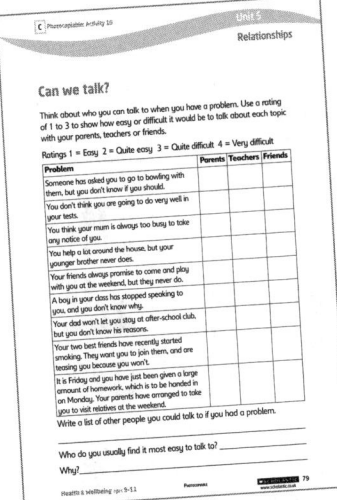

Health & Wellbeing ages **9-11**

Introduction

- Self-evaluation sheets – one for each unit.

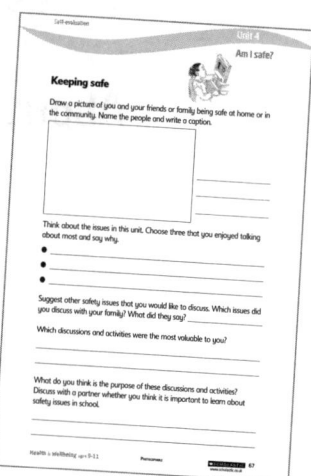

- Interactive activities – Three activities to accompany each unit for whole-class and group discussion and completion. The discussion surrounding the interactive activities is often more important than the *score* and therefore some of the activities do not have a scoring mechanism.

- Photos – Many of the units have photos to stimulate further discussion.

- Templates, cards and illustrations – Additional resources to develop greater understanding of unit concepts, and facilitate individual and group feedback.

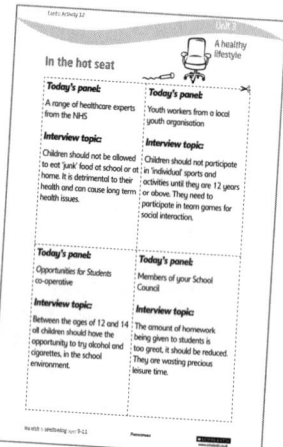

- Children's booklets – one for each unit to reinforce unit objectives and skill development and provide an opportunity for reflection and self-assessment. These can also be used to stimulate home involvement.

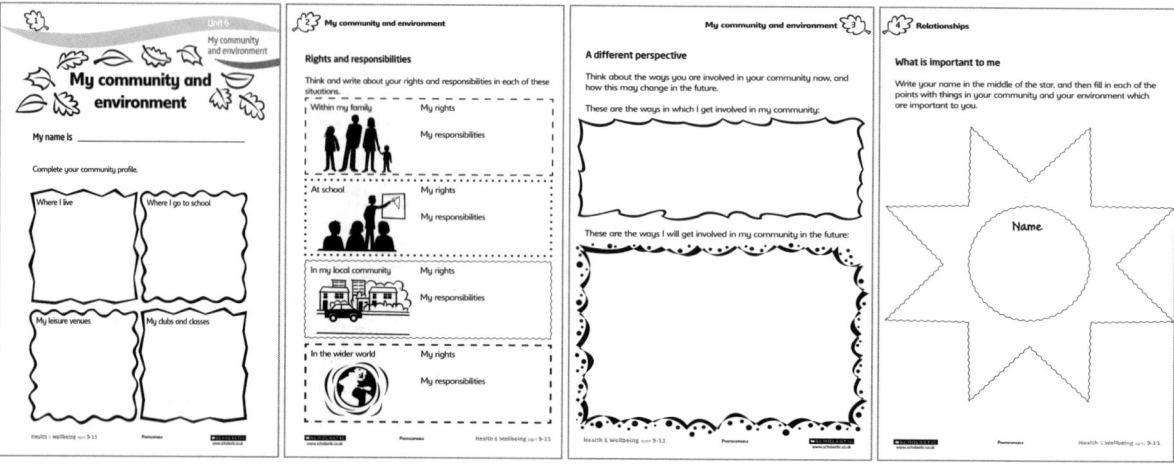

Health & Wellbeing ages 9-11

Introduction

PSHE in the classroom

Setting the scene: A whole school approach

It is important to see PSHE in the classroom within the context of the ethos and environment of the whole school and its community. This is reinforced in the *Every Child Matters* legislation and the National Healthy Schools Programme. A 'Healthy' school has:
- A safe environment which supports and extends learning for all
- A supportive ethos which promotes confidence and self-reliance in all
- An extended community which is dynamic and supportive
- A 'child-centred' and integrated PSHE curriculum.

Spiral development – Revising the topics

When planning PSHE for the whole school, throughout the year there is a need to develop and revisit topics as children grow and mature. This spiral development of topics encourages children to revisit these important topics and develop skills in the PSHE areas of study which are age-appropriate, but which continue to challenge their thinking and understanding.

Let's talk – Starting with talk

Circle time is an important opportunity for children to begin an exploration of topics, question their own knowledge and articulate what they want to learn and to take away from each activity or exploration. It is an ideal way to begin each unit or activity. A range of questions has been provided for an introductory circle time discussion of each unit. Teachers are encouraged to use this opportunity to allow children to ask questions of themselves and of others, to ensure that all children remain engaged. When exploring a topic of activity, it is important to:
- Be inclusive; try to involve all children in the questioning and discussion, giving particular thought to children for whom English is an additional language.
- Redirect comments and questions, so that a number of children can respond.
- Use positive statements, and encourage children to use positive rather than negative talk (for example: *I can find out about,* rather than *I don't think I will ever be able to*).
- Summarise the discussion, sometimes during the discussion, and at the end of the session.
- Make your objectives explicit, and encourage children to do the same.

Getting involved – Using children's own work

It is important that children see themselves at the centre of the PSHE topics and have the opportunity to relate each topic to their own lives, both now and in the future. It is therefore suggested throughout the activities that children talk about and illustrate their responses to questions and comments and that these verbal and illustrated responses are shared with their peers and throughout the school, and that non-judgemental reactions from others are solicited and discussed. These personalised responses will also give teachers insights into children's thinking and perceptions.

Introduction

Reflection – Questions and prompts

Reflecting on learning and group or class interaction regularly, at the end of sessions or units, is helpful to both the teacher and the children. It give teachers an opportunity to understand how children tackled the task, the strategies they used, how they interacted in small or large groups and what they think they achieved; it also allows children the opportunity to articulate what they achieved, how they worked individually or in groups and what they still want to achieve. Questions and prompts such as these can focus on the task, the strategies, the group dynamics etc and can be aimed at individual and/or group reflection:

- What strategies did you use during the activity?
- Did you achieve your goal?
- Did you get better at anything?
- Do you understand the topic better?
- Did you find it useful to work with a partner/group?
- How well did your group work?
- Could your group work better in the future?
- How do you feel about the topic?

Evaluation and assessment

The purpose of evaluating and assessing children's learning is to plan for continued skill and personal development. Where possible, both children and teachers should be involved in the assessment process, and this should include both informal and formal assessment. There are many opportunities to informally assess children's work and contributions throughout the activities. Extending this assessment to interpersonal and behavioural skills will help children become self-confident and increase their maturity. Children can use the following type of continuum to self-evaluate or peer-evaluate interpersonal and behavioural skills:

I encourage others to give their opinions on the topic.

I listen to others.

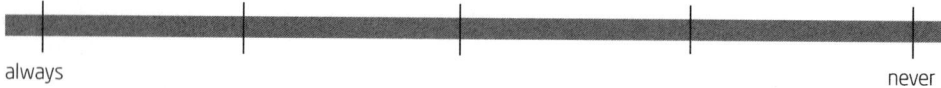

Child A participates in group discussions.

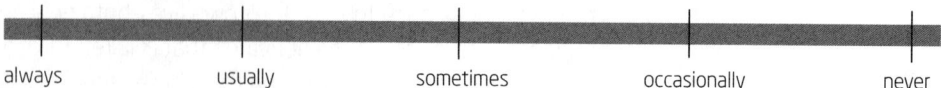

Health & Wellbeing ages **9-11**

Introduction

About the series

Health & Wellbeing is a comprehensive multimedia resource that combines the requirements of *Every Child Matters* and the guidelines for PSHE and citizenship into a manageable programme of work. It is designed to enable teachers to engage in these topics throughout the primary school years.

Health & Wellbeing (ages 4-5) Foundation units	Early Learning Goals (Personal, social and emotional development)	Every Child Matters	SEAL
This is me	Be confident to try new activities, initiate ideas and speak in a familiar group Have a developing awareness of their own needs, views and feelings and be sensitive to those of others	Enjoy and achieve	Good to be me Going for goals! Changes
All the things I need	Have a developing awareness of their own needs, views and feelings and be sensitive to those of others	Enjoy and achieve Achieve economic well-being	Changes
My feelings	Respond to significant experiences, showing a range of feelings when appropriate Be confident to try new activities, initiate ideas and speak in a familiar group	Enjoy and achieve	New beginnings Getting on and falling out Good to be me
Thinking about others	Have a developing awareness of their own needs, views and feelings and be sensitive to those of others Understand that people have different needs, views, cultures and beliefs, that need to be treated with respect	Enjoy and achieve	New beginnings Getting on and falling out Good to be me
My body	Dress and undress independently and manage their own personal hygiene	Be healthy	Changes
Healthy me	Dress and undress independently and manage their own personal hygiene	Be healthy	Changes
Be safe!	Consider the consequences of their words and actions for themselves and others	Stay safe	Say no to bullying
My friends and family	Form good relationships with adults and peers Work as part of a group or class, taking turns and sharing fairly	Make a positive contribution	Getting on and falling out Say no to bullying Relationships
Playtime	Form good relationships with adults and peers Consider the consequences of their words and actions for themselves and others	Make a positive contribution	Getting on and falling out Say no to bullying Relationships
My community	Have a developing awareness of their own needs, views and feelings, and be sensitive to those of others Have a developing respect for their own cultures and beliefs and those of others Work as part of a group or class, taking turns and sharing fairly	Make a positive contribution	Changes
Right and wrong	Understand what is right and wrong and why Consider the consequences of their words and actions for themselves and others Work as part of a group or class, taking turns and sharing fairly	Make a positive contribution	Changes

Introduction

Health & Wellbeing (ages 5-7) KS1 units	National Curriculum	Every Child Matters	SEAL
Who I am	Developing confidence and responsibility and making the most of their abilities	Enjoy and achieve Achieve economic well-being	Good to be me Going for goals! Changes
Feelings	Developing confidence and responsibility and making the most of their abilities	Enjoy and achieve	New beginnings Getting on and falling out Good to be me
Keeping healthy	Developing a healthy, safer lifestyle	Be healthy	Changes
Keeping safe	Developing a healthy, safer lifestyle	Stay safe	Say no to bullying Changes
Good relationships	Developing good relationships and respecting the differences between people	Make a positive contribution	Getting on and falling out Say no to bullying Relationships
Looking after our environment	Preparing to play a role as active citizens	Make a positive contribution	Changes

Health & Wellbeing (ages 7-9) Lower KS2 units	National Curriculum	Every Child Matters	SEAL
All about me	Developing confidence and responsibility and making the most of their abilities Developing good relationships and respecting the differences between people	Enjoy and achieve Make a positive contribution	Good to be me Going for goals! Changes Relationships
My feelings	Developing confidence and responsibility and making the most of their abilities Preparing to play an active role as citizens	Enjoy and achieve Make a positive contribution	Getting on and falling out Say no to bullying Good to be me Relationships
Healthy me	Developing a healthy, safer lifestyle	Be healthy Make a positive contribution	Changes Relationships
My safety	Developing a healthy, safer lifestyle	Stay safe Make a positive contribution	Say no to bullying Going for goals!
My relationships	Developing good relationships and respecting the differences between people	Make a positive contribution Enjoy and achieve	New beginnings Getting on and falling out Say no to bullying Relationships
My community and environment	Preparing to play a role as active citizens Developing confidence and responsibility and making the most of their abilities	Make a positive contribution	Changes Relationships

Introduction

Health & Wellbeing (ages 9-11) Upper KS2 units	National Curriculum	Every Child Matters	SEAL
Discovering myself	Developing confidence and responsibility and making the most of their abilities Developing good relationships and respecting the differences between people Preparing to play a role as active citizens	Enjoy and achieve Make a positive contribution Stay safe	Good to be me Going for goals! New beginnings Changes Relationships
Good days and bad days	Developing confidence and responsibility and making the most of their abilities Developing good relationships and respecting the differences between people Preparing to play an active role as citizens	Enjoy and achieve Make a positive contribution	New beginnings Getting on and falling out Say no to bullying Going for goals! Good to be me Relationships
A healthy lifestyle	Developing a healthy, safer lifestyle Developing confidence and responsibility and making the most of their abilities	Be healthy Make a positive contribution	Changes Good to be me Relationships
Am I safe?	Developing a healthy, safer lifestyle Developing confidence and responsibility and making the most of their abilities	Stay safe Make a positive contribution	Say no to bullying Going for goals!
Relationships	Developing good relationships and respecting the differences between people Preparing to play an active role as citizens	Make a positive contribution Enjoy and achieve	New beginnings Getting on and falling out Say no to bullying Going for goals! Relationships
My community and environment	Preparing to play a role as active citizens Developing confidence and responsibility and making the most of their abilities Developing good relationships and respecting the differences between people	Make a positive contribution Enjoy and achieve	Changes Relationships

How to use the CD-ROM

System requirements

Minimum specification:
- PC with CD-ROM drive: Windows 98 or higher
- Processor: Pentium 2 (or equivalent) 1000 MHz
- RAM: 512 Mb
- Graphics card and colour monitor capable of displaying 24-bit colour graphics at a resolution of at least 1024x768 pixels.

- Mac with CD-ROM drive: OS X and above
- Processor: G3 1000 MHz
- RAM: 512 Mb
- Graphics card and colour monitor capable of displaying 24-bit colour graphics at a resolution of at least 1024x768 pixels.

Getting started

The *Health & Wellbeing* CD-ROM program should auto-run when you insert the CD-ROM into your CD drive. If it does not, use My Computer to browse the contents of the CD-ROM and click on the *Health & Wellbeing* icon.

From the start-up screen there are four options: Click **Credits** to view a list of acknowledgements. If you would like to register an interest in the series, click on **Registration** and follow the prompt. You must then click on **Terms and conditions** to read the terms and the licence conditions. If you agree to these terms then click **Continue**: this will take you to the **Main menu**.

Main menu

Each of the six *Health & Wellbeing* units contains up to six different types of resource, which can be accessed as follows:
- Firstly click on the links to access the six *Health & Wellbeing* units.
- Click on **Interactive activities** to view or complete any interactive activity provided.
- Click on **Photocopiables** to view and print the photocopiable resources.
- Click on **Photos** to view and print these resources for some units.
- Click on **Templates, cards and illustrations** to view or print these pdf resources.
- Click on **Children's booklet** to view or print this 'reflection' resource.

Introduction

Interactive activities

Each of the units has three interactive activities, which are referenced in the unit text. It is suggested that the interactives be viewed on an interactive whiteboard, a computer screen or a data projector and shared with the whole class for discussion in the first instance. When an activity has been completed it is checked by clicking on the **Check answers** button. Any incorrect answers are returned to their original position by clicking on the **Try again** button which gives children the opportunity to correct initial incorrect responses. To revisit the activity, click on the **Back** button.

Photocopiable resources

To view or print the photocopiable resource pages (photocopiables, templates, cards, illustrations and children's booklets), click on the required title on the list. To view photocopiables or templates as a full page, click **Actual size** and then the page icon with four arrows around it, at the top of the screen. To print the selected resource select **Print**. To return to the **Menu**, click **Back**.

Viewing and printing photos

Photos initially appear in a frame with whiteboard tools. To see the photo at full screen, click on the **Actual size** button. To print an image, click on the **Print** button. To navigate between images, use the **Next** and **Previous** buttons.

Whiteboard tools

Four tools have been provided for annotating photos and templates: a pen, highlighter, speech bubble and eraser. When using the speech bubble, use the keypad to add text to the bubble. The tools will continue to be available if the photograph or template is displayed, or can be minimised if required. To show the tools palette again, click on the **Tools** icon.

CD navigation

- **Back:** click to return to the previous screen.
- **Help:** click to go to **How to use this CD-ROM**.
- **Home:** click to return to the **Main menu**.
- **Quit:** click to close the program.

Technical support

For all technical support queries, please phone Scholastic Customer Services on 0845 603 9091.

Unit 1
Discovering myself
Unit planner

Aims of the unit
Children can develop a stronger sense of their own identity and place in the world around them if they have the self-confidence and self-esteem to help them to investigate both their individuality and their place within a social setting. As they approach the final years of their primary schooling they will be facing new challenges, including the emotional aspects of puberty and the transition to secondary school. The aim of this unit is to develop the children's self-esteem in order to equip them with the confidence to handle internal and external pressures positively.

> **Key concept**
> Develop skills of intrapersonal behaviour, enabling them to think about their own identities; begin to understand how personal values have an important role to play in making difficult choices.

Learning outcomes
By the end of this unit:
- All the children should be able to identify and describe their individual persona including some strengths and weaknesses. Additionally they will begin to realise that other people will also have views on this and be able to point out personal qualities that they themselves may be too modest to realise. Most should also be able to recognise that there are more similarities between people than there are differences.
- Most will be able to identify and explain how their behaviours are influenced not only by their own personalities but also by the social contexts within which they find themselves. Some may also be able to describe accurately the pressures that others put on them, and what the consequences of bowing to these pressures might be, now and in the future.
- Some may be able to reflect on and evaluate their achievements and strengths in all areas of their lives and recognise their own worth. They will understand how behaviours and characteristics are influenced by family and cultural expectations and begin to recognise and challenge stereotypical images. They will be able to demonstrate effective ways of resisting external pressures, including negative pressure from their peers.

Curriculum links
PSHE
- Developing confidence and responsibility and making the most of their abilities
- Developing good relationships and respecting the differences between people
- Preparing to play an active role as citizens

Every Child Matters
- Enjoy and achieve
- Make a positive contribution
- Stay safe

SEAL themes
- Good to be me
- Going for goals!
- New beginnings
- Changes
- Relationships

> **Vocabulary**
> Characteristics, self-esteem, advertisement, persuade, peer pressure, role model, responsibilities, body image, achievements, gimmicks, media, influence, agony aunt, consequences, inner voice

Unit planner

Unit 1
Discovering myself

Organisation
The activities in this unit may be worked through in the order in which they appear or in another order to suit your ongoing planning. All of the activities are introduced as part of whole-class teaching. The follow-up activities include a range of individual, paired, small-group and whole-class work.

Resources
You will need the following resources to complete the activities in this unit:

Core photocopiable pages
Page 25 My autobiographical poem
Page 26 Little eyes upon you
Page 27 Responsible behaviour
Page 28 Self-evaluation sheet

CD-ROM
Interactive activities:
- Personal qualities quiz
- Body image advice
- Why didn't you do your homework?

Photocopiables:
- My autobiographical poem (support)
- My autobiographical poem (extension)
- Little eyes upon you (support)
- Little eyes upon you (extension)
- Responsible behaviour (support)
- That's irresponsible! (extension)

Plus core photocopiables as above

Photos:
Children and young people

Templates, cards and illustrations:
- Negative thoughts
- Family traits
- 'Eat Joosy Frooty Choos'
- How to say 'No'
- Peer pressure scenarios
- Little Eyes Upon You
- How to be responsible
- Sentence stems

Children's booklet:
Discovering myself

Evaluation
The self-evaluation sheet and children's booklet allow the children to reflect upon how much they have learned about themselves during the unit. It is suggested that each child responds to the evaluation by writing, or in some cases drawing, answers according to his or her ability. Some guidance from an adult helper may be necessary.

Watch points
Be aware of the different lifestyles and values that pupils learn from their homes and communities and how they might influence their opinions. The nature of the material in this unit may raise sensitive issues. The activities should be undertaken in a climate of safety where pupils know that their opinions will be listened to and not ridiculed. To this end, ground rules which encourage the children to listen and behave sympathetically should be set, and reinforced, before, during and after the lessons.

The references to puberty are included to link with, and not replace, schools' existing programmes for health and sex education.

Unit 1
Discovering myself

Let's talk

Circle time and thinking activities

The question boxes provide ways to get the children thinking and talking about the factors that contribute to making them who they are. It is important to encourage the children not simply to think about their body image, but to focus instead on their personal qualities and values.

1 What is the first thing you notice when you meet a new person? What characteristics of a person can't be seen? Is the way in which we judge people always fair or sensible? How would you want people to judge you?

2 What do you think the expression 'See yourself as others see you' means? Do you think that is possible? How easy is it to describe your strengths? Is it easier to focus on your weaknesses? Is everyone aware of their own strengths and weaknesses?

3 Do you ever compare yourself with other people? How can it hurt you to compare yourself with other people? How can it help you? What is self-esteem? What is the difference between high self-esteem and low self-esteem? What are some causes of low self-esteem?

4 What it is that makes a family? Do you need parents and children for family? Is a blood relationship necessary to belong to a family? Do you have to live together all the time to be a family? Has the nature of families changed over the years?

5 What is an advertisement? Where do you see or hear adverts? Who makes them? What are they trying to do? Are advertisers misleading young people by creating fantasy worlds? Are adverts only used to sell things? What else do adverts try to persuade people to do?

6 What is peer pressure? If a friend tried to pressure you into smoking cigarettes, what would you say? Why do people have trouble saying 'no' to friends? When someone suggests doing something you don't feel right about, what are some things you can do, besides just saying 'no'?

7 What is a role model? Who are your role models? Are role models always people in the public eye? What kinds of people make good role models? Do we always choose good role models? What kind of responsibilities do role models have? Are you anybody's role model?

8 Why do so many people wish they looked differently? Why do we think we should look a certain way? Where does our notion of an 'ideal' body come from? Why is there so much focus in our society on body image? Who controls the images we see?

9 Do your parents sometimes expect you to act grown up, but then treat you like a child? Do you sometimes act like a young adult and at other times act as a child? Do you think being a teenager is easy or hard?

10 What does it mean to describe someone as a 'responsible' person? What responsibilities do people of your age have? Do you know someone who is very responsible? Have you ever let somebody else take the blame for something you did? How did the other person feel about it?

18   Health & Wellbeing ages 9-11

Unit 1
Discovering myself

Activities

Activity 1: What do I admire?

Start by asking the children who they admire. Write the names of the people they suggest on the whiteboard. Are they all celebrities? Suggest that there could be 'everyday' people that we also admire, and include some of these on the list. What is it about each person that they admire? Make a list of the characteristics mentioned and work with the children to organise them into physical characteristics or personal qualities. Which are the most important?

Ask the children *What makes a good person?* Make a class list of words pupils think help define 'a good person'. Ask the children to write down the three qualities they think are most important and the three they think are least important, with reasons. Decide upon a class consensus of the six most important and the six least important.

Return to the list of people they admire. Which show the personal qualities the children considered to be most important? Do any show the qualities considered least important?

Display the interactive activity **Personal qualities quiz.** Give the children time to discuss each question in small groups, before discussing as a whole class. Conclude by asking the children to write about someone they admire, describing that person's best qualities and why they admire him or her. The completed work could be illustrated with pictures (from magazines or newspapers; drawings; paintings; clip art or digital photos).

Activity 2: The best of me

Display pieces of paper, with the name of a child on each, around the classroom. Invite the children to write a thoughtful and positive comment on five of the papers. Give examples of appropriate comments (for example, 'You tell good jokes') before they begin. Ask the children to describe how it felt to look for positive attributes in their peers and how they felt about sharing those. Once the children have read their comments, ask them to write a paragraph describing how they felt about the comments, and if they learned any new positive things about themselves.

Explain that it is often easier to recognise the achievements of others than to acknowledge our own strengths. Ask the children to think carefully about some things about themselves of which they are proud. They should write down at least three things they have achieved: one at home, one at school and one in the wider community (the extended family could be included here).

When they have finished, group the children into pairs and give each pupil three minutes to tell their partners about their achievements. Encourage some pupils to tell the rest of the class about the achievements of their partners.

Conclude by explaining that although it's important to be proud of your achievements, sometimes it's important to keep quiet about your strengths (be modest). For example, if another child is struggling with their reading, it's not very tactful to tell them that you can do it better!

Unit 1
Discovering myself

Activity 3: My self-esteem bucket

Ask the children to imagine their self-esteem as a bucket of water. We start out feeling good about ourselves, and our buckets are full. Every time someone puts us down, it's like punching a little hole in the bucket, and our self-esteem leaks out. Ask the children to think of ways people punch holes in each other's buckets and ways we can plug up the holes and raise self-esteem.

Ask the children to think of words we use every day that can punch holes in our 'self-esteem buckets'. For example: *no, can't, won't, never, if, maybe*; these are negative words because they can stop us before we attempt a task. They can lower our self-esteem when we use them as an excuse for not doing something that will challenge us.

Show the **Negative thoughts** illustrations from the CD-ROM. Read each caption with the class and explain how these negative thoughts punch holes in our 'self-esteem buckets'. Encourage the children to suggest ways in which that person's self-esteem can be raised with a positive statement.

Ask each child to print their name vertically down the left-hand side of a sheet of paper, writing each letter separately. They then think of a positive, self-descriptive word or phrase to match each letter of their name. Conclude by asking them to write a descriptive paragraph or story about themselves, using the words or phrases they have selected.

Activity 4: My family's identity

Begin the activity by displaying a selection of business cards you have collected. Ask the children what information they can learn about a person by reading their professional business card (for example, business name, what the business does, logo, and address).

Invite the children to make a number of 'My family' cards to show what is important to each member of their families, and makes them unique. Reiterate that a family unit can come in many different forms, and can include carers and extended family. The cards should show their family name surrounded by symbols (similar to business logos) that represent their talents, goals, skills, and characteristics. Allow time for the children to share and explain their finished cards with the class.

Display the **Family traits** template and demonstrate its use by filling it in using yourself as an example. Consider each characteristic, and write down a word or two in the 'ME' column that describes you, and the family member you share the attribute with, in the next. Ensure that you write 'no one' in some of the spaces. When the children have understood the process, give them individual copies of the template to complete.

Give each child a copy of the core photocopiable page 26 **My autobiographical poem**, or the support or extension version on the CD-ROM, and ask them to create their poem. Encourage them to illustrate it if they wish. Make a display of the poems.

Activities

Unit 1
Discovering myself

Activity 5: What influences me?

Ask the children to photograph or collect examples of advertisements from different media (for example, newspaper, magazine, television, billboard, football pitch, taxi, and so on). Display the adverts and invite the children to discuss their common features. Highlight the ways in which adverts use gimmicks such as: peer pressure; using 'new and improved' to describe the item; using celebrities, or 'cute' babies and children; cartoon characters; catchy jingles, and so on. Ask the children to give examples of each gimmick.

Display the '**Eat Joosy Frooty Choos'** poster from the CD-ROM. What are the advertisers trying to say about eating their sweets? Do the children agree with the messages the adverts are trying to put across? Ask them to draw their own versions of the advert, using facts about the dangers of eating too much sugar. For example, instead of smiling children with sparkling white teeth they could draw them with decayed or missing teeth.

Collect adverts for products that will appeal to children (for example, fast food, shoes, toys, sweets, computer games). With the class, analyse the target audience and whether the adverts work. Invite the children to recall any 'must-have' toys from the past few years. What made these toys so popular? Their answers might include: media promotion; everyone else has got one; if it's difficult to get hold of, those who have it feel really special.

Extension
Invite the children to invent a new toy and devise some imaginative ways to get the toy onto every child's wish list.

Activity 6: Who influences me?

Ask the children if anyone has ever said to them 'No one will ever know', 'I do it all the time and I've never been caught', 'Everyone else is doing it', 'Don't be a chicken' or other similar phrases. When have they heard such phrases? Have they used them themselves? Why are these phrases used?

Explain that sometimes our friends, or other people of a similar age, exert pressure on us to behave in a certain way; this is called 'peer pressure'. Discuss positive and negative peer pressure and ask for examples of both types. Impress upon the children that there are ways to say 'no' to peer pressure without losing face. Discuss each step in the **How to say 'No'** poster and give and ask for specific examples.

Divide the class into groups of four or five. Give each group a **Peer pressure scenarios** template. Invite them to choose a scenario, giving them the opportunity to practise and role play it to the rest of the class. Discuss each role play with the class. What was the scenario? What words did the pressure group use? Was it a positive or negative peer pressure situation? How did the person being pressured respond? Could anything have been done differently? Elicit varied suggestions and responses from a range of children.

Conclude by asking the children to design 'Say no' posters for a classroom display.

Health & Wellbeing ages 9-11

Unit 1
Discovering myself

Activities

Activity 7: Who do I influence?

Play a game of 'Simon says', increasing the pace until many of the children are eliminated. Explain that what makes the game tricky is that it is easier to copy actions first, without always listening to instructions. We see someone put their hands on their heads and immediately do the same, without listening for the magic words 'Simon says'. We all find it easy to copy someone else. How many times have we heard someone say: 'But he did it first...'? What do adults usually reply?

Ask the children if any of them have younger siblings who copy what they do. Emphasise that being a role model to a younger person is quite a responsibility. It is not only younger brothers and sisters who copy them, but also younger pupils at school. It is through copying them that they learn to be polite and behave appropriately. Sometimes they might also copy inappropriate words and actions; they are too young to think whether something is right or wrong. They see an older pupil whom they admire doing it, so they copy that person.

Display and discuss Kimberly Sedlacek's poem **Little Eyes Upon You** from the CD-ROM. Then ask the children to complete the core photocopiable page 27 **Little eyes upon you**, or the support or extension version on the CD-ROM.

Conclude by reminding the children that they do have an influence on the behaviour of younger children and should therefore act responsibly at all times.

Activity 8: How do I look?

Begin by reminding the children that there are billions of people living on the Earth, and each one of us has physical traits that make us unique. Some of us are small; some of us are big; some are fair, some are dark; some are girls, some are boys. Ask the children to look around the room at their classmates; look at all the differences between the people in just this one room!

Collect magazine images that reinforce the 'ideal' body images for women and men. In small groups, the children should make montages of these images and superimpose the words 'Love your body, not theirs'. Discuss how images in magazines have often been touched up or airbrushed, so they are not even real photos of people.

Describe a scenario where aliens travelling through space come upon a deserted space station where they find a pile of discarded magazines. Ask the children to imagine that they are the aliens and write a description of a typical earthling, based on what they've seen in the magazines.

Remind the children that even though they are not aliens, they might have a picture in their mind of an 'ideal' body image. What advice would they give to 10- and 11-year-olds who are unhappy about the way they look? Use the **Body image advice** interactive activity to discuss appropriate advice, and reach a consensus in organising them in order of usefulness.

Activities

Unit 1

Discovering myself

Activity 9: We're all changing

Display the photos **Children and young people** from the CD-ROM. Ask the class which of the children are approximately the same age as themselves. How do they know? Ask them how an 11 and a 7-year-old differ. Prompt them to mention physical changes, behavioural changes, relationships at home and at school, leisure pursuits, demands of schoolwork, and so on. Write their suggestions on the whiteboard. Then ask if all 11-year-olds share the same traits. What might be different about the way individuals look, think and feel?

It is normal for children of their age to think that their experiences are different from those of others. They are approaching a stage when they begin to grow into young adults. This is called 'puberty'. Many of the changes are physical, and have been discussed during sex education. Emphasise that their emotional development is also proceeding very quickly; some of them may find their moods change from day to day. Discuss the best and worst points about growing up.

Conclude the session by asking the children to write a letter to an agony aunt telling her about the problems an imaginary 10-year-old is having. Explain that they can sign the letters with a 'nom de plume' and post them in a box you have provided. Use some of the letters in subsequent sessions and ask the children if they can think of any answers to the problems.

Activity 10: Taking responsibility

Explain that in your career as a teacher you have met many pupils who have not done their homework. (Joke that none of them are in your present class!) Display the interactive activity **Why didn't you do your homework?** Consider each excuse in turn and ask the children what could have been done to make the excuses unnecessary (for example, 'Keep your homework away from your little brother!') Use their suggestions to add their own speech bubble and text to each scenario. Discuss their contributions and the differences between excuses and reasons. Emphasise that excuses are rarely valid; we all need to be responsible for our own actions.

Display the **How to be responsible** poster and discuss each point, asking the children to think of examples to illustrate each one. Emphasise that they often have to make choices and these can be responsible or irresponsible; each choice will have a consequence.

Arrange the children into small groups and give each a copy of the core photocopiable page 28 **Responsible behaviour**, or the support or extension version (**That's irresponsible!**) on the CD-ROM. Each group should discuss the rules and then decide upon an example of someone who *did not* follow the rule, and what the consequences could be. After the groups have reported back, hold a discussion about classroom responsibility. What are the children's responsibilities? What are the adults' responsibilities? What are the consequences of being irresponsible? What are the rewards of being responsible?

Health & Wellbeing ages 9–11

23

Unit 1
Discovering myself

Activities

Activity 11: My inner voice

Ask the children to imagine they can hear what others say about them. Ask: *What kind of things would you like/not like them to say about you?* Explain that other people are not the only ones who talk about us. Everyone has an 'inner voice'. Can the children explain what you mean by this? Elicit that your inner voice is how you speak to yourself, or your 'self-talk'.

Emphasise that the most important thing about your inner voice is that you are the only person that can control it. Ask the children: *If you are at the controls of your self-talk, will you let in positive thoughts or negative thoughts?* Invite them to give examples of both positive and negative self-talk that they could use in a variety of situations (for example, before a school test, looking in the mirror). Reiterate that positive self-talk is an important key to success.

Ask the children which things about themselves they can change and which ones they can't. Which of these would a positive person concentrate on? Finally, give each child a piece of paper and tell them to make three lists: a list of things they do really well; a list of things they'd like to know or do better; and a list of positive and realistic things they could do to achieve some of their aims.

Activity 12: Where to next?

Invite the children to reflect back on their first day at primary school. How did they feel? What do they remember most? How did their parents feel? Were they worried about anything? If so, what? Ask them if they have any of the same feelings about their move to secondary school. Consider ways in which their secondary schools may be different from their primary school. Which of the differences are exciting? Which might be a bit unnerving?

Prepare a number of cards with completed sentences using the **Sentence stems** template. (Make more than one copy of each sentence stem.) Shuffle the cards (face down) and pass one to each child. Give the children time to think about their sentence stem, and complete the thought in their own way. Invite them to read their thoughts aloud, and help them to appreciate that many of their fears, concerns and questions are shared by their peers.

Conclude by giving the children an opportunity to make a display which shows what they have most enjoyed and achieved at primary school. Remind them to include both curricular and extra-curricular activities. Invite the primary liaison teacher from the receiving secondary school to come and see the displays.

Children can now complete the self-evaluation sheet or the children's booklet for the unit.

C Photocopiable: Activity 4

Unit 1

Discovering myself

My autobiographical poem

Complete these sentences to write a poem about yourself.

I am _____

Who was born in _____

The child of _____

Yes I am _____

Who loves _____ and _____ and _____

And hates _____ and _____ and _____

Remember, I am _____

Who feels _____

Who fears _____

Who wishes for _____

So now you know me

I am _____

Health & Wellbeing ages 9–11

Unit 1

Discovering myself

Photocopiable: Activity 7 C

Little eyes upon you

1. **Little ones watch and listen to you.**
   Give an example of something you do or say in school that would be a good influence upon younger children.

   Give an example of something someone might do or say in school that would be a bad influence upon younger children.

2. **Little ones do what you do.**
   Give an example of something adults do at home that would be a good influence upon children.

   Give an example of something that adults might do at home that would be a bad influence upon children.

3. **Little ones want to be like you.**
   Give an example of one of your personal characteristics that you would be proud for a younger child to copy.

Let's help Dad bring in the washing.

C | Photocopiable: Activity 10

Unit 1

Discovering myself

Responsible behaviour

Read these rules for being responsible. After each rule, write an example of someone who *did not* follow the rule and describe the consequences of their irresponsible actions.

1. When you agree to do something, do it. Don't blame others for something you have done or haven't done.

   _____
   _____

2. Don't rely on adults to remind you where you're supposed to be or what you're supposed to be doing.

   _____
   _____

3. If somebody trusts you to borrow or take care of something, take care of it.

   _____
   _____

4. If somebody tells you something in confidence, keep it to yourself.

   _____
   _____

5. Don't put things off. When you have a job to do, do it.

   _____
   _____

Unit 1

Self-evaluation

Discovering myself

Discovering myself

Name _____

Before you complete this sheet, think carefully about all of the activities you have done. Look at the displays in the classroom and check back on some of the work in your books and folders.

I have learned more about _____

_____

I would still like to learn more about _____

_____

_____

I enjoyed _____

_____

because _____

_____

I did not really enjoy _____

_____

because _____

_____

I did best when _____

_____

I think I need more help when _____

_____

The most important thing I learned about myself was _____

_____

28　**SCHOLASTIC**　　　**Photocopiable**　　　Health & Wellbeing ages 9–11
www.scholastic.co.uk

Unit 2

Good days and bad days

Unit planner

Aims of the unit
Children can develop a stronger sense of their own identity and place in the world around them if they have the self-confidence and self-esteem to help them understand and control their own emotions and recognise the impact these have on other people. Additionally they need to be aware of the way in which emotionally-charged situations may lead to confrontations, and how these can be reconciled without resorting to violent words or actions. The aim of this unit is to develop the children's understanding of powerful emotions and to equip them with coping strategies, especially as they confront the strong emotions associated with approaching puberty.

> **Key concept**
> Develop skills of intrapersonal behaviour which will enable them to recognise and control their own emotions for their own benefit, and that of others.

Learning outcomes
By the end of this unit:
- All of the children will be able to identify and describe the nature of their emotions and the responsibilities that they have for ensuring that they are controlled. Additionally they should be beginning to realise that they sometimes need to take the emotions of others into account, and aim to deal with confrontation maturely.
- Most should be able to identify strong emotions and explain how to manage them. They should be able to give reasons for the onset of such emotions and choose from a range of strategies when dealing with confrontation.
- Some may be able to recognise some strong emotions and identify ways of managing their emotions positively. They may also know when and how to help others in dealing with emotions. They should recognise that all the emotions they experience are normal, and it is in the way which they are expressed that is important.

Curriculum links
PSHE
- Developing confidence and responsibility
- Developing good relationships and respecting differences
- Preparing to play an active role as citizens

Every Child Matters
- Enjoy and achieve
- Make a positive contribution

SEAL themes
- New beginnings
- Getting on and falling out
- Say no to bullying
- Going for goals!
- Good to be me
- Relationships

Unit 2
Good days and bad days

Unit planner

> **Vocabulary**
> Mood, emotions, honesty, stress, pressures, determination, goals, courage, caring, behaviours, trust, trustworthy, truth, tact, consequences, attitude, disappointment

Organisation
The activities in this unit may be worked through in the order in which they appear or in another order to suit your ongoing planning. All of the activities are introduced as part of whole-class teaching. The follow-up activities include a range of individual, paired, small-group and whole-class work.

Resources
You will need the following resources to complete the activities in this unit:

> **Core photocopiable pages**
> Page 38 Name that feeling
> Page 39 What can I say?
> Page 40 Courage profile
> Page 41 Self-evaluation sheet

> **CD-ROM**
> *Interactive activities:*
> - What would a trustworthy person do?
> - Choose your words carefully
> - Consequences of anger
>
> *Photocopiables:*
> - Name that feeling (support)
> - Name that feeling (extension)
> - What can I say? (support)
> - What can I say? (extension)
> - Courage profile (support)
> - Courage profile (extension)
> Plus core photocopiables as above
>
> *Photos:*
> Body language
> *Templates, cards and illustrations:*
> - Mr Nobody
> - Memory chart
> - How stressful is that?
> - Shooting star
> - What is courage?
> - Showing we care
> - What would you say?
> - Great expectations
> *Children's booklet:*
> My feelings

Evaluation
The self-evaluation sheet and children's booklet have been designed to allow the children to reflect upon how much they have learned about emotions during this unit. It is suggested that each child responds to the evaluation by writing, or in some cases drawing, answers according to his or her ability. Some guidance from an adult helper may be necessary.

Watch points
The nature of the material in this unit may raise sensitive issues. The activities should be undertaken in a climate of safety where children know that their opinions will be listened to, and not ridiculed. To this end, ground rules which encourage the children to listen and behave sympathetically should be set, and reinforced, before, during and after the lessons. Make it clear, however, that no one is being asked to disclose anything and that the classroom is not the best place to discuss very personal problems. Ensure that you, any additional adults in the classroom and the children themselves are aware of the relevant school policies and procedures.

Unit 2

Good days and bad days

Let's talk

Circle time and thinking activities

The question boxes provide ways to get the children thinking and talking about all the things that contribute to making them who they are. It is important to encourage the children not simply to think about what they look like or what their name is, but to focus instead on what they are like as people.

1 Do you ever have big mood swings? Describe what they're like. Describe a time you had a hard time coping with the way you felt about something. What made it hard? What did you do about it? Is there something you could have done that would have made it easier?

2 What is wrong with lying? Do you trust people who lie? Do you care if your friends lie? Can lying ruin a friendship? How? Has that ever happened to you? Would you trust somebody who lies or cheats or steals? Do you consider yourself to be an honest person?

3 What kinds of things make you sad? How do people show sadness? What do we do that makes other people sad? How might we respond to the death of a pet? Would you treat the death of a pet goldfish in the same way as a cat or dog?

4 What is stress? Is life more stressful as you get older? What pressures are you under? Is all stress bad? What is the difference between good and bad stress? What is the most serious stress you are feeling? Is this caused by yourself or others?

5 Does attitude have anything to do with success? Do your expectations about yourself affect what you will achieve? Why do some people give up and stop trying? Do you ever do that? Is it better to set high goals that are challenging, rather than low goals that are easy?

6 What is courage? How have you demonstrated courage in your life? What does 'having the courage to be yourself' mean? What is moral courage? What things in your life require moral courage? Is courage something you are born with, or can you develop it?

7 What is a caring person? Would it bother you if your friends thought you were uncaring? How do you know when somebody really cares? How does it feel when people show that they care about you? Are you a caring person? In what ways are you a caring person?

8 How do you know if you can trust someone? What is a trustworthy person? In what way are you a trustworthy person? Do your parents trust you? What might you do that could make your parents stop trusting you? What difference would that make to your life?

9 Should we always tell the truth? Are there any times when it is correct to tell a small lie? What kinds of things are often hard to say? Should you tell the truth, even if it will hurt somebody's feelings?

10 What happens when we get angry? How can you tell when you are getting angry? Does getting angry make things better or worse? What are some good ways to get rid of your anger? What are some good ways to handle someone else's anger?

Health & Wellbeing ages 9–11

Unit 2
Good days and bad days

Activities

Activity 1: What kind of day did you have?

Show the **Body language** photos from the CD-ROM one at a time. Discuss what each person may be feeling or thinking and what kind of day they might have had. Ask each child to choose a photo and write a diary entry for that person, describing their mood and what happened during the day to make them feel that way.

Invite the children to reflect upon the fact that they might sometimes feel in a bad mood for no particular reason. Explain that this 'moodiness' is a sign that they are growing up, and that their emotions are sometimes out of their control. If they think about it, they can probably recognise their bad moods and the reasons for them. Ask if any of the children would like to describe some of the things that put them in a bad mood. Some children may have strategies for coping with these moods and be willing to share them. Distribute copies of the core photocopiable page 38 **Name that feeling**, or the support or extension version on the CD-ROM, and ask the children to complete them individually.

Ask the children who they talk to when they are feeling down, and how that person helps. Work with the children to research local and national sources of help for a variety of emotional problems that children may experience.

Activity 2: Truth and honesty

Ask the children if they have ever heard the saying, 'Honesty is the best policy'. What does it mean? Ensure that they understand that honesty is not just about telling the truth, but also involves not cheating or stealing, and having the courage to own up when you have done something wrong. Ask them if they think cheating is another form of lying, and to give reasons for their opinions.

Discuss times when the children may have damaged something by accident, or not done something they had promised to do. Did they own up or keep quiet, hoping that no one would notice? Tell them that there was a poem that their great-grandparents may have learned at school and read the poem **Mr Nobody** from the CD-ROM together. Discuss the poem and some of the old-fashioned language and concepts. Do they think that, even though the poem is an old one, the message is the same today? Work with the class on a shared writing activity to update parts of the poem to make it more relevant to modern children.

Ask the children if they agree with the proposition that things are often made much worse by not owning up and being honest can make life a lot easier. Have any of them got any examples that they are willing to share? Conclude by asking the children for examples of dishonesty that they particularly dislike and examples of honesty that they really appreciate.

Activities

Unit 2
Good days and bad days

Activity 3: Sharing feelings about death and loss

Death is a natural part of life, but it is important to be sensitive while choosing how and when to introduce the topic. Ask the children to think about someone they used to know well (give some examples of children or teachers who have moved to another school or area). Ensure that the children realise that they can keep these thoughts private and not share them with the rest of the class, but be prepared for some children to discuss friends, relatives or even pets that have died. Tell the children a true story about a pet that died. Tell them how you felt, what made you feel better and how you feel now when you think about the pet.

Remind the children that it is alright to feel sad that the person they are thinking of is no longer with them, but that this activity is about remembering happy times. On the whiteboard, demonstrate how to make a memory chart using one of the children or teachers you mentioned earlier. Write the person's name in the middle of the board and surround it with words, phrases and pictures that remind you and the class of that person. Give each child a copy of the **Memory chart** template and ask them to complete it. Again emphasise that they may want to keep their work private but they can share it with you, other adults in the school, parents, relatives or friends if they would like to.

Explain that when others have had distressing news, it is difficult to know what to say. In pairs, ask the children to discuss a situation they have experienced or know of, or suggest one for them. Give each child a copy of the core photocopiable page 39 **What can I say?** or the support or extension version on the CD-ROM, and ask them to complete it individually.

Activity 4: Stress and pressure

Copy the **How stressful is that?** cards from the CD-ROM and give a set to each group of three children. Ask each group to discuss the cards and choose the three situations they feel are most stressful and the three they feel are least stressful. Ask each group to feed back to the rest of the class and elicit the fact that different people find different things stressful.

Work with the class to decide which three situations are most likely to cause them stress and brainstorm how to deal with each stressful situation in turn. Extend this activity by asking the groups to return to their original three 'most stressful situations' and role play ways of dealing with them. Invite some groups to perform their role plays.

Explain that stress and pressures are a normal part of life and approaching puberty and secondary schools can be increasingly stressful. What matters is not how much stress they have, but how well they keep it in perspective and handle it.

Discuss the kinds of pressures they feel as family members, as school children and as 10- and 11-year-olds. How do they deal with those pressures? Suggest that the children write down any pressures they are feeling at school as they occur, and put them in a 'Stress box' in the classroom. Check the box regularly, working together to deal with the pressures in a positive, helpful manner.

Unit 2
Good days and bad days

Activity 5: Overcoming difficulties

Begin by telling Aesop's fable, *The Crow and the Water*. A crow, nearly dead from thirst, finds water in the bottom of a deep pitcher, but cannot reach it with his beak. He desperately tries to reach it, before giving up in despair. Then he comes up with a plan, and drops stones into the pitcher, pebble by pebble. Slowly the water level rises until he can quench his thirst. Discuss the lesson that this fable teaches us; that with enough planning and determination, it is possible to achieve what at first seemed impossible.

Ask the children to tell the class about times when they succeeded at something which was very challenging. Brainstorm a list of the skills and attitudes they needed to reach their goals. Talk also about some of the barriers that got in the way and the self-discipline needed to overcome them. Ask the class to share some of their 'big goals'; what they would like to achieve by the time they are 19. Explain that these goals should be attainable, and that it's a good idea to have smaller goals along the way. Give each child a copy of the **Shooting star** template. They should write their big goal in the star at the top and five smaller goals in its tail.

Conclude by reminding the children that Aesop's crow could have given in, but he knew that his life depended on getting at the water. When we are trying to overcome our difficulties, if we can't find an obvious solution, we must step back and come up with a fresh idea.

Activity 6: Courage

Tell the children the story of Rosa Parks, or any other person who showed great moral courage. Ensure they understand that courage doesn't mean that you are ready to fight someone. It means that you are willing to do what you believe is right. Sometimes this is not easy if other people want you to do something else. Ask them to consider the **What is courage?** poster from the CD-ROM. Did Rosa Parks show examples of any of these behaviours?

Challenge the children to research other courageous historical figures and complete the core photocopiable page 40 **Courage profile**, or the support or extension version on the CD-ROM. Display the leaflets that they have produced and encourage the other children to read them. Ask some individuals or groups to make a presentation to the class about the people they have chosen. What have they learned from the people they selected?

Role play some situations which require taking a courageous stand against a group or an individual. After each improvisation, discuss the important principle or issue that was at stake. How well did the individuals demonstrate the courageous behaviours listed on the **What is courage?** poster? What could he or she have done better?

Complete this activity by asking the children to find pictures of courageous people and make a montage for a classroom display. Encourage them to find quotes and sayings about courage and bravery which could also be displayed.

Activities

Unit 2

Good days and bad days

Activity 7: Caring

Ask the children what it means to be a caring person. Ask for specific examples of behaviour that a caring person displays. Compare their list with the **Showing we care** poster from the CD-ROM.

As a class, decide on the basic ingredients for a 'caring recipe' by writing a list of words and phrases associated with caring on the whiteboard. In pairs, ask the children to write the method (for example, they might begin, 'Take a generous heart...'). When the children have written and illustrated their 'caring recipes' include them in a 'Recipes for caring' book.

Brainstorm ways to make your school environment more caring. Create a list of recommendations for the children to take a caring role in the school community. They might choose to be 'reading buddies' or 'playground buddies'. Before they do so, ensure that they understand that such a position will require them to prioritise their time so that they can fulfil their commitments and undertake some special training before they start.

Conclude by imagining the class had won £20,000 to be used to help other people. What would they do with it, and why?

Activity 8: Trust

You can trust me

I am honest

I am reliable

I have the courage to do what is right

I am a good friend

Display the **You can trust me** poster (in margin) on the whiteboard. Ask the children to think of as many examples of each characteristic as they can, and write them on the whiteboard. Are there other behaviours that show that people can be trusted? Add them to the list. Ask the children to design and produce posters for each behaviour, and display these around the school.

Ask the children whether we should start off trusting people, and only stop trusting if they prove that they're not trustworthy. Or should we be cautious and not trust them until they prove themselves trustworthy? What are the advantages and disadvantages of each position? Make sure that they understand the child protection issues involved.

Discuss the potential problems with the breakdown of trust occurring between: children and teachers; children and parents; children and each other; teachers and parents; adults and other adults. Encourage the children to give examples to back up their opinions.

Work through the **What would a trustworthy person do?** interactive activity. Discuss the pros and cons of each answer, before reaching a class consensus. Finish the session by saying that if an individual's answers showed that they were perfectly trustworthy, they probably wouldn't be a trustworthy person! Ask the children to tell you what they think you meant by that remark.

Health & Wellbeing ages 9-11

35

Unit 2

Good days and bad days

Activity 9: Expressing opinions

Explain to the class that sometimes saying what you really think can be very difficult. It can be risky to say what you really feel because you might be disappointed by the reply, you might get into trouble or you don't want to upset or offend people.

Arrange the class into pairs and distribute one **What would you say?** card to each pair. Encourage the children to discuss their scenario, working together to decide the best approach in the situation. What should they say? Bring the class back together and ask for volunteers to demonstrate what they said and did.

Explain that as a general rule, honesty is the best policy. However, the truth is not always pretty, and sometimes blunt honesty can be hurtful. If we are saying something that could upset a person, we should try to be tactful. Tact, though truthful, is not insulting or rude. By emphasising the positive, and offering solutions for the negative, we can provide tactfully honest answers that do not offend anyone.

Give the children some examples of tact and ask if they can think of any others. Work together to complete the interactive activity **Choose your words carefully** by adding their own speech bubbles and text, giving tactful responses. Discuss the various responses.

Activity 10: Exploring anger

Write the word 'Anger' on the whiteboard. Ask the children to describe some behaviours which result from uncontrolled anger. Display the interactive activity **Consequences of anger** and discuss each scenario. What do children think is happening in each scenario? What is the behaviour being displayed? What are the possible consequences of these behaviours? Many different suggestions may result from the discussion; these discussions and justification of suggestions are as important as the results of the activity.

The scenarios in order are: (1) getting into a fight; (2) planning revenge; (3) pretending not to be bothered; (4) running to bedroom in anger; (5) saying nasty things to friends; (6) screaming and swearing at a sibling; (7) slamming doors; (8) taking anger out on parents or carer; (9) thinking nasty thoughts about others; (10) throwing and smashing things. The suggested *consequences of anger* are: It is an agressive display – 1, 7, 10; It spoils relationships – 2, 5, 6, 8; It is bottled up inside and causes misery – 3, 4, 9.

Ask the children if anything has made them angry in the past week, and discuss some of the situations in a 'no blame' environment. Introduce the idea that feeling angry is fine; it's how we deal with it that can be wrong (for example, by lashing out uncontrollably). Anger has three parts: the thoughts, the feelings and the behaviours; if the first two parts are controlled, the third might be eliminated, or manifested positively. For example, someone may push in front of them in the dinner queue. What do the children think? Responses will probably range from 'How dare he!' to 'Perhaps he's had no breakfast'. Classify each thought as to how likely it is to make you feel angry.

Explain that the angry thoughts might make their muscles tense, their breathing rapid, and might make them feel like they're going to explode.

Teach the children how to relax and calm down with simple relaxation exercises. Demonstrate how to breathe in slowly, stretching and tightening muscles, as you count to five. Hold your breath a few seconds before you count back to one again, release the air and relax your muscles. Once we are relaxed we can handle anger in positive ways.

Activities

Unit 2

Good days and bad days

Activity 11: A problem shared

Ask the children if they have ever felt embarrassed because they didn't know something, couldn't do something or made a mistake. Encourage them to discuss some of these situations, how they felt and what they did about it. What was the reaction of other people? Discuss why it can be hard to admit we don't know something, or have made a mistake, and what the consequences might be if we never ask for help.

Arrange the children into groups of five or six and ask them to focus on a problem that one of them remembers or invents. Ask them to develop two role plays around the problem: the first depicts others reacting negatively to the problem; the second shows others reacting sympathetically. Each group should present their work to the rest of the class.

Work with the class to brainstorm different kinds of help children can get from others. Focus on particular groups of helpers such as school staff, friends, siblings, parents or carers. Extend this activity by making posters showing different kinds of problems and potential helpers.

Ask the children to imagine that someone needs help but is embarrassed to ask for it. Challenge them to write a short story about the person with two different endings: the first when he or she didn't ask for help and the second when he or she asked for help and got it.

Activity 12: Always look on the bright side of life

Show a glass which is half full (preferably of a clearly visible, colourful liquid). Ask the class if the glass is half-full or half-empty. They should quickly conclude that it could be either one. Explain that how you see things (your point of view) is called your 'attitude'. The glass can be either half-empty (negative attitude) or half-full (positive attitude).

Organise the class into groups of three, and allocate each a **Great expectations** card. After discussing their scenario, they should write a sentence or two from a negative perspective (for example, 'It seemed like the end of the world because...'). They then write a sentence or two from a positive perspective.

When the children have completed the task, they should share their discussions with the class. Focus their thoughts on what the person had expected to happen and how realistic these expectations were. What positive strategies could be used to deal with the disappointment? Conclude the unit by saying that every day has the potential to be a good and, in some cases, a great day for you. The children may have heard the expression, 'Have a nice day!' Suggest that your class changes this greeting to 'Make it a great day!' Ask them for ways in which they can do this, and make a poster for the classroom.

Children can now complete the self-evaluation sheet or children's booklet for the unit.

Health & Wellbeing ages 9–11

37

Unit 2

Good days and bad days

Name that feeling

Think about the following situations. For each, write how you feel and how you would deal with the situation.

1. What do you feel when you're blamed for something you didn't do?
   What is a good way of dealing with that feeling?

2. What do you feel when someone keeps fouling you on the football pitch?
   What is a good way of dealing with that feeling?

3. What do you feel if you are expecting to see a friend, and he or she backs out at the last moment for no good reason?
   What is a good way of dealing with that feeling?

4. How do you feel when you succeed at something that was really difficult?
   What is a good way of dealing with that feeling?

5. What do you feel when your favourite team keeps losing?
   What is a good way of dealing with that feeling?

6. What do you feel when a teacher praises your work?
   What is a good way of dealing with that feeling?

7. What do you feel when get low marks in a test because you haven't revised?
   What is a good way of dealing with that feeling?

8. What do you feel when your parents say you can't do something that you really want to do?
   What is a good way of dealing with that feeling?

C Photocopiable: Activity 3

Unit 2

Good days and bad days

What can I say?

Write some kind words to comfort this child in distress.

Health & Wellbeing ages 9-11

Unit 2

Good days and bad days

Courage profile

Choose a famous person who showed courage.

Use the library and the internet to find out the answers to as many of these questions as you can.

- What is your courageous character's name?
- Why is your courageous character famous?
- When was your courageous character born?
- Where did your courageous character live for most of his or her life?
- Was this a small village, a town or a city?
- What were your courageous character's parents' occupations?
- Did your courageous character have any special kind of talent?
- What was your courageous character's job?
- What did your courageous character want the most? Why?
- What world issues was your courageous character passionate about?

Use what you found out to write a short information leaflet about your courageous character.

Self-evaluation

Unit 2

Good days and bad days

Good days and bad days

Name _____

Before you complete this sheet, think carefully about all of the activities you have done. Look at the displays in the classroom and check back on some of the work in your books and folders.

I have learned more about _____

I would still like to learn more about _____
_____

I enjoyed _____

because _____
_____

I did not really enjoy _____

because _____
_____

I did best when _____

I think I need more help when _____
_____

The most important thing I learned about my feelings was _____
_____

Health & Wellbeing ages 9–11

Unit 3
A healthy lifestyle

Unit planner

Aims of the unit
Children can develop a stronger sense of their own identity and place in the world around them if they have the self-confidence and self-esteem that help them to be healthy. As they approach the final years of their primary schooling, they are facing new challenges to maintain healthy lifestyle habits as their bodies and emotions change, and additional stresses and external pressures are experienced.

> **Key concept**
> Develop and maintain healthy lifestyle habits; learn how we can keep our bodies healthy now, and in the future.

Learning outcomes
By the end of this unit:
- All the children should be able to explain why it is important to make choices to develop a healthy lifestyle. They can identify some factors that affect emotional health and well-being.
- Most should understand how to take care of their bodies, particularly as they approach puberty. They will be able to make judgements and decisions and can list some ways of resisting negative peer pressure around issues affecting their health and well-being.
- Some may be able to reflect on and relate to the changes which are affecting their bodies and emotions in the health and well-being areas of their lives. They will be able to demonstrate effective ways of resisting external pressures, including negative pressure from their peers.

Curriculum links
PSHE
- Developing a healthy, safer lifestyle
- Developing confidence and responsibility and making the most of their abilities

Every Child Matters
- Be healthy
- Make a positive contribution

SEAL themes
- Changes
- Good to be me
- Relationships

PE
- Knowledge and understanding of fitness and health: pupils should be taught how important it is to be active; to recognise and describe how their bodies feel during different activities.

Science
- Sc2: Life processes and living things – Life processes 1a; Humans and other animals 2b,

Literacy
- Writing a diary
- Writing a procedure

> **Vocabulary**
> Healthy, unhealthy, lifestyle, stress, fitness, hygiene, carbohydrate, protein, dairy, nutrition, balance, strength, flexibility, leisure, drugs, allergy, responsibilities, expert, prevention

Unit 3
A healthy lifestyle

Unit planner

Organisation
The activities in this unit may be worked through in the order in which they appear or in another order to suit your ongoing planning. All of the activities are introduced as part of whole-class teaching. The follow-up activities include a range of individual, paired, small-group and whole-class work.

Resources
You will need the following resources to complete the activities in this unit:

Core photocopiable pages
Page 51 Staying healthy
Page 52 Nutrition labels
Page 53 Leisure time
Page 54 Self-evaluation sheet

CD-ROM
Interactive activities:
- Healthy lifestyle quiz
- How do they rank?
- Saying 'yes' or 'no'

Photocopiables:
- Staying healthy (support)
- Staying healthy (extension)
- Nutrition labels (support)
- Nutrition labels (extension)
- Leisure time (support)
- Leisure time (extension)
Plus photocopiables as above
Photos:
- Different sports
- Leisure time

Templates, cards and illustrations:
- Food diary
- Healthy food pyramid
- Food and drink advertising
- Why exercise?
- All different
- Personal health
- Positive and negative responses
- Stress metre
- More responsibilities
- In the hot seat

Children's booklet:
My healthy lifestyle

Evaluation
The self-evaluation sheet and children's booklet have been designed to allow the children to assess how much they have learned about keeping healthy during this unit. It is suggested that the child responds to the evaluation by writing, or in some cases drawing, answers according to his or her ability. Some guidance from an adult helper may be necessary.

Watch points
Be aware of the different lifestyles the children experience at home. Remember that children may not have the choice to eat healthily at home, and that they may not want to discuss this. Also, some children may be responsible for family meals without much help or guidance, and may be embarrassed to talk about what they are able to provide. However, point out that, when eating school dinners, they can make healthier choices. Be aware of any obesity issues in the classroom, and tailor discussion accordingly. Remember that religious and cultural differences may determine food choices and involvement in fitness activities, also religious rituals when discussing 'Looking after yourself'.

Before embarking on discussion of puberty and the male and female reproductive systems, refer to the schools Sex Education Policy and be sure children are mature enough to enter into the discussion. If necessary, place children in same-sex discussion groups.

Unit 3
A healthy lifestyle

Let's talk

Circle time and thinking activities

The question boxes will help facilitate the development of communication and participation skills and provide ways to get the children thinking and talking about the issues pertaining to the development of a healthy lifestyle. It is important to encourage all children to share their contribution with the group.

1 Do you think you are healthy? Do you know healthy people? What does being healthy mean? What are healthy things to do? What can affect our health? How do others help us stay healthy? Are there different kinds of health – physical, emotional, social?

2 What healthy food and drink do you enjoy? Why should you eat healthy food? How can you find out what foods are healthy and what are unhealthy? What do you know about the different types of foods? Do you know about the food pyramid?

3 Can you name ten healthy foods? How do you know they are healthy? Do you know what is in the foods you eat? How can you find out? Is it important to know what is in your food? Do you think advertisers tell you how healthy their products are?

4 Is it easy to always eat healthy foods and drink? What things influence what you eat and drink? Are you influenced by advertising? What else influences your food choices? What would you eat if you could choose all the time? Would it be good for you?

5 Who is the fittest person in the class? Why? How do you know if someone is fit? Is it important to be fit? Why do we need to be fit? Do you enjoy doing things that make you fit? Do you feel good when you are doing fit activities?

6 What do you do when you get home from school? How much leisure time do you have? Do you wish you had more? What would you do with the extra time? How do you use your leisure time? Do you all do the same things with your leisure time?

7 How have you changed since you started primary school? Has anything changed about your body in the last year? Was it a big change or a small change? Have you all changed in the same way? What are the differences between your bodies and teenagers' bodies?

8 Who looks after your body? Does anyone else look after your body? Is it important to look after your own body? What will happen if you don't have a shower every day, clean your teeth, and wash your hair? Would it worry you? Would it worry other people?

9 Do you know people who smoke/drink? Is it okay to do these things? Do you know what the law says about smoking? Do you know what the law says about drinking? Do you think these are fair laws? Why do you think some drugs are illegal? Is this right?

10 Do you get worried and stressed about exams? What else makes you worried or stressed? Do you all get stressed by the same things? Why do you think that is? Do you think your parents and carers have worry and stress? Is it different to yours?

Unit 3
A healthy lifestyle

Activities

Activity 1: A balancing act

Start by asking the children if they have ever tried to juggle three or four balls. If possible, have one or two sets of balls for volunteers to have a try in class. Why is it hard to keep the balls in the air and moving around? Explain to the children that this can be what it is like managing healthy lifestyle issues.

Ask the children what issues (juggling balls) they need to juggle in health. Arrange the children into small groups and give each a health card that you have prepared: 'Physical health'; 'Emotional health'; 'Social and spiritual health'. Ask them to brainstorm the factors which affect that health type, in each case thinking of the positive and negative aspects. Prompt the children to think about issues of stress (exams, moving house) and physical issues (carrying heavy backpacks). Does everyone have the same lifestyle? What are the similarities and differences? At the end of the session ask the children to come up with a definition to the question, 'What is a healthy lifestyle?'

Provide the children with a copy of the core photocopiable page 51 **Staying healthy**, or the support or extension version on the CD-ROM. Ask them to think about and complete the sheet, considering the most important issues for each person. Invite volunteers to tell the rest of the class what they have written.

Display the interactive activity **Healthy lifestyle quiz** on the whiteboard. Give the children time to discuss each question in small groups or with a partner. At the end of the session discuss their responses and ask if any children have questions or want to make any comments.

Activity 2: Healthy food

Begin by reminding the children that a healthy and balanced diet is essential for a growing body. This means eating a variety of foods from the food pyramid. Snacks and takeaway foods are all right in moderation, but usually contain too much sugar, fat and salt. Show the **Healthy food pyramid** illustration from the CD-ROM and discuss each of the food groups. Ask the children how many servings they should have of each food group, before telling them. Why is it important to eat fibre? Why is it important not to eat too much fat or sugar? Do they eat foods from each group? Do they eat too much from certain groups?

Ask the children to complete a **Food diary** template for the last two days, reminding them to be honest about all the things they have eaten. They should then discuss their diary with a partner, to make suggestions about how they could each improve their diet. Remind the children of the need to be tactful; suggest phrases such as 'I suggest that...' or 'Do you think you could...'. Conclude by asking the children to write two or three sentences on the benefits of healthy food.

Extension
In groups, ask the children to look through recipe books and brainstorm 'healthy snacks'. Ask each group to design their own healthy snack and to write and display their recipe.

Unit 3

A healthy lifestyle

Activities

Activity 3: How healthy is it?

How many children are involved with the preparation of, or shopping for, food? As they get older they should become increasingly involved in taking responsibility for their diet. Be aware that some children may already have responsibility for some of these tasks.

Display the interactive activity **How do they rank?** on the whiteboard. Discuss the first scenario with the class and make a class selection as to how healthy the featured foods are. Encourage children to discuss and justify their food positioning. What other foods could they add? Show each of the other scenarios in turn, asking the children to discuss them in pairs. After a couple of minutes ask for a pair to feed back and discuss their conclusion. Do this for each scenario (the discussion and repositioning of foods is as valuable as a correct answer).

Explain to the class that the majority of foods we buy (all tinned, bottled and pre-prepared foods, but not fresh foods) have labels that tell us what they contain. Remind the children that it is important to be aware of the ingredients. Two of the most important things to look for are the fat and sugar content, both of which should be lower than 10g per 100g. Salt or sodium is another one to watch and it should be less than 50mg.

Arrange a range of tinned and dry goods for the children to look at and talk about. Give each child a copy of the core photocopiable page 52 **Nutrition labels**, or the support or extension version on the CD-ROM, to complete. Ask them to look particularly at the nutrition values for 100g and then look at the recommended serving, if there is one.

Activity 4: What to eat

Ask the children to think about food advertising and brainstorm the different forms of advertising (television, magazines, newspapers, the internet, out and about on buses and taxis). Which media do the children think is most/least effective? In groups, give the children copies of the **Food and drink advertising** template and ask them to fill it in.

Were there many common foods? Discuss why these might have been remembered. Were the advertisements targeted at their age group? Were they foods they particularly like? Do the children remember the **Eat Joosy Frooty Choos** advertisement from Unit 1?

Collect and show examples of foods which fall into the 'junk' food category. Why are these called junk food? Ask the children to look at the nutritional information for the foods. Encourage them to keep their own 'junk food diary' for a week and bring it to school for a class discussion.

Explain that we all eat junk food sometimes; it is when it is eaten all the time that it becomes a problem. What are the alternatives to junk food? How often should they eat junk food? What strategies could they use to cut back on the amount of junk food they eat?

46

Health & Wellbeing ages **9-11**

Activities

Unit 3
A healthy lifestyle

Activity 5: Why exercise?

Show the **Why exercise?** template and discuss the scenarios (one person feeling good after exercising, the other feeling lethargic). Place the children in pairs; give half of the class one scenario and the other half the other. Ask them to discuss and write how each person feels, or what they are thinking, in the thought bubbles.

As a whole class, discuss the benefits of exercise. As the children make suggestions, write a list on the whiteboard. Benefits of exercise include:
- Exercise is important for healthy development of bones and muscles.
- Exercise makes it easier to maintain a healthy weight, as it burns up fat.
- Regular exercise helps lessen the risk of heart disease and some forms of cancer.
- Weight-bearing exercise such as brisk walking or jogging helps to keep bones strong.
- Exercise helps you sleep, as your body becomes physically tired and it can alleviate stress.
- Exercise gives you a 'feel good' factor due to the endorphins which are released into your blood stream and they give you energy.
- Exercise and sport can improve your 'teamwork' skills and help your confidence.

Ask the children to record on a piece of paper each family member and how much exercise they do each week. They should record the types and duration of each activity. Then ask them to transfer the information to a graph and compare their graph with their partner. Make sure the children are positive with each other, particularly where less exercise is being done.

Display the **Different sports** photos from the CD-ROM. Talk about the parts of the body used by each and the fitness requirements of each sport or exercise. For example, some require balance (gymnastics, horse riding), some require strength (sprinting, including in a wheelchair, swimming), and some require flexibility (badminton, netball and football). However, most require a combination of two or more of these attributes.

Activity 6: Leisure activities

Begin by reminding the children that many people use their leisure time to keep fit, playing a sport or exercise. This often means participating in activities with others and provides opportunities for social interaction. Other people use their leisure time differently and sometimes alone. Display the **Leisure time** photos on the whiteboard and discuss each one.

Ask the children to think about their leisure activities: when and where they do them, with whom and how they feel about them. Invite them to discuss these with a partner. Make a mind map by adding the activities on the whiteboard, with information about when and where they are done, and with whom. Encourage the children to express how they feel about the activities and add some 'feelings' words to the mind map.

Give each child a copy of the core photocopiable page 53 **Leisure time**, or the support or extension version on the CD-ROM, and ask them to record some of their frequent leisure activities and some which they participate in less often. Encourage them to include as much detail as possible (including their feelings). Using their sentences, create a classroom display. Do the children think that leisure is important? Why?

Extension
Invite the children to make a list of all the leisure facilities (for all ages) in your community. Ask: *Are there enough leisure facilities? If not, what you could do about it?*

Unit 3

A healthy lifestyle

Activity 7: Your changing body

Our bodies are changing all the time. Ask the children to explain how they have changed since they were babies, and since they started primary school. They should consider how they looked, how they communicated, what they needed and what they could do on their own. Ask them to bring in photos of themselves as babies and when they started school. Display these on a wall as a continuum and add a digital photo of each child now.

Changing bodies can cause problems for children and they may become self-conscious, particularly if: they have weight problems; they are the first to display signs of puberty; their voice begins to break or they have a problem with acne. Discuss these issues with the children and encourage them to 'feel good' about their changing bodies. Use the **All different** cards on the CD-ROM to begin the discussion if necessary.

If appropriate, ask the class to brainstorm their knowledge of the male and female reproductive systems, and the changes that occur in each sex. Arrange the children into groups and ask them to discuss the similarities and differences between female and male changes at puberty. Display a Venn diagram on the whiteboard and suggest that they use this to record their findings.

Give the children the opportunity to write statements or questions about issues or concerns they have about puberty and the changes taking place in their bodies. Place these in a box and randomly select some to be discussed either in class or small groups.

Activity 8: Looking after yourself

Explain that we all have responsibility for looking after our bodies, but that there are some things we can't do ourselves. Divide the class into small groups and give each group a set of **Personal health** cards from the CD-ROM.

Each group must firstly divide the cards into 'Things I can do to look after my body' and 'Things with which I need help in looking after my body'. They should then discuss each card in the first group and discuss what they do and what they could do better,

Ask the children to collect photos of personal hygiene products from newspapers and magazines. These should be displayed, in groups relating to the body part for which they are intended. Ask the class to list all the parts of the body which need their attention. Don't forget: any special needs, such as children with glasses; any changing needs with the onset of puberty; any occasional needs, such as skincare when on holiday in the sun. Ask the children to write their own personal care routine chart, showing the routines they do every day, every week and occasionally.

Can the children remember the issues from the 'Things with which I need help in looking after my body' cards? Ask class members who have any of these health problems to talk about their special needs; how are they met and who helps them? Alternatively discuss some more common health issues for children such as diabetes, asthma or an allergy, and some less common issues such as kidney disease.

Activities

Unit 3

A healthy lifestyle

Activity 9: Saying 'no'

Ask the children what things they know they should not put into their bodies: food and drink (alcohol); drugs (discuss the difference between legal drugs and illegal drugs); air and smoke. Encourage the children to say what they think in class; explain that it is a good time to explore these issues.

Display the interactive activity **Saying 'yes' or 'no'** on the whiteboard. Ask the children to reflect on each question and then agree on an answer. Encourage them to make judgements in each instance and tell the class why they think that.

Have the children tried alcohol or cigarettes (and if they are mature and the school policy allows – drugs) at home, or with their mates? Do they think it is okay to drink a little or a lot; is it 'bad' for you? Do they think it is okay for secondary school children? Arrange the children into groups and allow three to five minutes to plan a role-play scenario which involves 'saying no' to a cigarette, an alcoholic drink or drugs. Each group presents their role play, and the class discuss the strategies used in the scenario to 'say no'. Make a class list of the strategies used by the class.

Give each group a **Negative and positive responses** template and ask them to pick an 'issue' from a hat. Give them time to discuss their issue and agree on some positive and negative responses to each. Ask each group to present one positive and one negative response to the class. Do the rest of the class agree with their responses?

Extension
Make a 'Being positive' display, use some of the 'positive responses' and add some personal 'positive statements' from the children, such as 'I can make good choices' or 'I make up my own mind'.

Activity 10: Stress less

Ask the children to name places, events or people who cause them stress, and list them on the whiteboard. Then ask them to give you places, events or people who provide the opposite reaction (keep them calm) and add these. Draw a 'stress metre' on the whiteboard – most stressful at one end and least stressful at the other end. Add a selection of the things which 'do' and 'don't' cause stress, discussing why they cause this reaction.

Give each child a copy of the **Stress metre** template and ask them to complete their own stress metre. Remind them that they do not need to share their work with anyone else, unless they want to. While the children are working on this, play a variety of music (some calm and restful and some strident and loud). Did the children notice the music? Did it have any effect?

How do the children feel when they are stressed? Remind them that there are positive aspects of stress – it can help us perform in games or at school. But too much stress will make us anxious and unable to perform our tasks effectively.

Ask the children to think about the consequences of stress. Do they lose their temper or yell at others? Is this a good way to react? Invite them to discuss one stressful situation with a partner and find an alternative, positive way to deal with it. Reassure them that there is no right way; it is up to each individual how they deal with each situation. Encourage them to share some of their positive strategies with the class.

Unit 3
A healthy lifestyle

Activity 11: Being more responsible

Invite the children to think back to when they were younger and just starting at primary school. Did they make many decisions about their health and fitness or their personal hygiene and care? Who made these decisions for them? Who did they depend on?

Ask the children to think about their lives now. Do they make more decisions about their health and fitness now? What decisions do they make? Does anyone help them make these decisions? Do they still rely on others for some health and fitness decisions? Do they expect changes when they go to secondary school?

Display the **More responsibilities** template on the whiteboard and discuss each of the categories with the class. Encourage them to think about all aspects of their daily lives, for example: choosing what they want for lunch when out with their family, where once mum or dad might have ordered for them; making purchasing decisions about shampoo and other products. Invite them to complete their own template.

Give the children the opportunity to create a display of digital photos which shows them making decisions now that they didn't make when they were younger. They could add captions explaining what the photo shows, and saying what they expect to happen in the future.

Activity 12: In the hot seat

Ask the children if they have watched a panel show where the audience ask questions to a group of 'experts'. These shows are often about current affairs, or important issues. If possible, show a short clip from a panel show.

Display the four **In the hot seat** cards from the CD-ROM to the class. Hold a class discussion to familiarise the children with the activity. One group will take the role of the panel of 'experts'; they must elect a 'chair' and then prepare themselves to each make a brief statement (all different) about the topic before finally taking questions from the class.

Remind the class that the 'audience' must ask direct questions, which are open-ended. They should avoid questions that can be answered with 'yes' and 'no' as this will limit the discussion. They should listen intently to the opening statements from the panel.

Give the panel time, in another room, to plan their opening statements and their strategies. They should prepare for questions they think they might get, but also devise strategies for 'deflecting' questions. The remainder of the class should discuss (in groups) the 'sorts' of questions which might be applicable to the topic.

Invite the panel to address the class. Conclude by asking the children to write down any issues which have been raised during the course of the unit, which have given them cause for thought.

Children can now complete the self-evaluation sheet or the children's booklet for the unit.

C Photocopiable: Activity 1

Unit 3

A healthy lifestyle

Staying healthy

Look at these pictures of healthy people. What do you think each one needs to stay healthy?

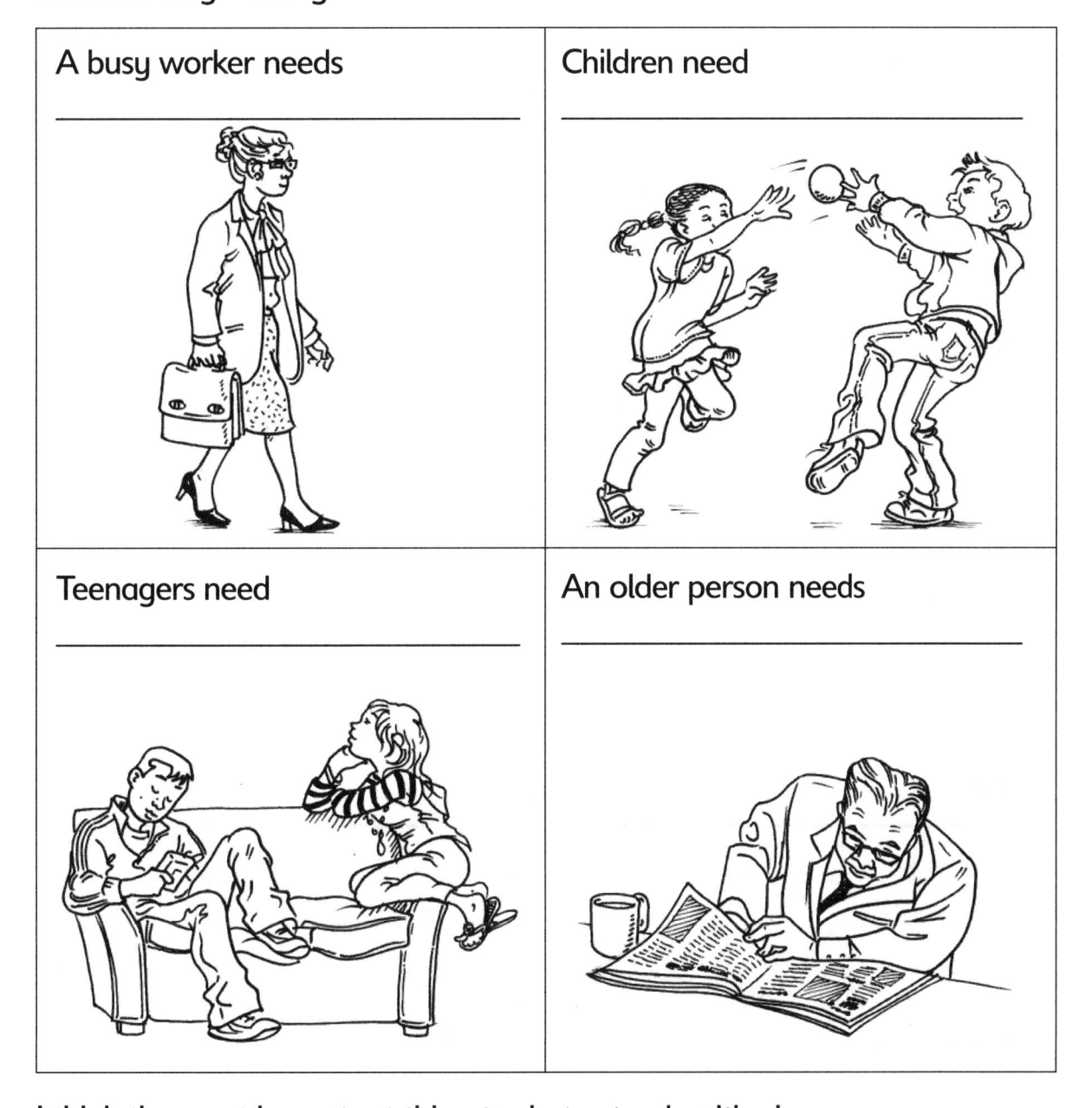

A busy worker needs _____	Children need _____
Teenagers need _____	An older person needs _____

I think the most important thing to do to stay healthy is _____

_____

because _____

Health & Wellbeing ages 9-11

Unit 3

Photocopiable: Activity 3 C

A healthy lifestyle

Nutrition labels

Choose two food products. Look at the nutritional information on each product and complete the boxes below.

Product _____
Per _____
Calories _____   Fat _____
Saturates _____ Salt _____
Sugars _____

Nutrition information	Quantity	Quantity per 100g
Energy		
Protein		
Carbohydrate		
Fat		
Fibre		
Sodium		

Product _____
Per _____
Calories _____   Fat _____
Saturates _____ Salt _____
Sugars _____

Nutrition information	Quantity	Quantity per 100g
Energy		
Protein		
Carbohydrate		
Fat		
Fibre		
Sodium		

- Is there too much of any ingredient?

- Is the quantity per 100g misleading?

- Is this a healthy food?

- Is there too much of any ingredient?

- Is the quantity per 100g misleading?

- Is this a healthy food?

C Photocopiable: Activity 6

Unit 3

A healthy lifestyle

Leisure time

In each box, write a leisure activity you do most weeks.

Write about each activity, saying when and where you do it and if you do it on your own or with other people.

Which one is your favourite leisure activity? Why?

_____ is my favourite leisure activity, because _____

_____

_____

What leisure activity do you really enjoy, but don't do very often? Why do you enjoy it? _____

_____

Health & Wellbeing ages 9-11   Photocopiable   53

Unit 3

Self-evaluation

A healthy lifestyle

Healthy living and me

Name _____

Draw a picture of you and your friends or family enjoying a healthy activity. Name the people and write a caption.

_____

Think about the issues in this unit. Choose three that you enjoyed talking about most and say why.

Suggest other healthy issues that you would like to discuss.

Which issues did you discuss with your family? What did they say?

Which discussions and activities were the most valuable to you?

What do you think is the purpose of these discussions and activities?

Discuss with a partner whether you think it is important to learn about healthy living issues in school.

Unit 4
Am I safe?

Unit planner

Aims of the unit
Children can develop a stronger sense of their own identity and place in the world around them if they have the self-confidence and self-esteem to help them to stay safe. Safe behaviours adopted in childhood lay firm foundations for children to behave in acceptable and risk-free ways in the future, and to resist pressure to do wrong. As they approach the final years of their primary schooling they will face new challenges and the aim of this unit is help them understand the judgements and decisions they need to make to handle pressures and remain safe.

> **Key concept**
> Develop and review concepts of safety and assessment of risk which will help keep them safe as they become more independent, now and in the future.

Learning outcomes
By the end of this unit:
- All the children should be able to identify and describe the potential risks facing them and can identify solutions. They can understand road safety rules and use them effectively. They should also know the people they could ask for help if they are in danger, and understand why rules keep them safe. They can identify ways of resisting negative peer pressure when it comes to issues concerning their safety and well-being.
- Most should be able to identify and explain managing risks in different familiar situations, and be able to understand the concept of individual responsibility for safety. Most should be able to predict confidently the consequences of their actions may be for themselves and others.
- Some may be able to reflect on and evaluate safety rules, and their own behaviour in safety situations. They may be able to demonstrate effective ways of resisting external pressures including negative pressures from their peers.

Curriculum links
PSHE
- Developing a healthy, safer lifestyle
- Developing confidence and responsibility and making the most of their abilities

Every Child Matters
- Stay safe
- Make a positive contribution

SEAL themes
- Saying 'no' to bullying
- Going for goals!

Geography
- Knowledge and understanding of patterns and processes: pupils should be taught to make observations about where things are located (for example, a pedestrian crossing).

Design and technology
- Working with tools, equipment, materials and components to make quality products: pupils should be taught to follow safe procedures for food safety and hygiene.

Science
- Health and safety: pupils should be taught to recognise that there are hazards in living things, materials and physical processes, assess risks and take action to reduce risks.

Maths
- Processing, representing and interpreting data

Literacy
- Writing a report

Unit 4
Am I safe?

Unit planner

> **Vocabulary**
> Safe, unsafe, accidents, safety, rules, frightened, danger, risk, scared, prevention, audit

Organisation
The activities in this unit may be worked through in the order in which they appear or in another order to suit your ongoing planning. All of the activities are introduced as part of whole-class teaching. The follow-up activities include a range of individual, paired, small-group and whole-class work.

Resources
You will need the following resources to complete the activities in this unit:

> **Core photocopiable pages**
> Page 64 Risks at home
> Page 65 Is it safe?
> Page 66 Danger!
> Page 67 Self-evaluation sheet

> **CD-ROM**
> *Interactive activities:*
> - What would a safe person do?
> - Sports safety equipment
> - Choose your words
>
> *Photocopiables:*
> - Risks at home (support)
> - Risks at home (extension)
> - Is it safe? (support)
> - Is it safe? (extension)
> - Danger! (support)
> - Danger! (extension)
> Plus core photocopiables as above
> *Photos:*
> - Road safety signs
> - Natural disasters
>
> *Templates, cards and illustrations:*
> - Safety web
> - Online chat
> - Still life
> - If, then
> - Constructing an advertisement
> - Be cautious
> - Natural disasters
> - Safety responsibilities
> - Safety at school
> *Children's booklet:*
> Am I safe?

Evaluation
The self-evaluation sheet and children's booklet have been designed to allow the children to assess how much they have learned about keeping healthy during this unit. It is suggested that the child responds to the evaluation by writing, or in some cases drawing, answers according to his or her ability. Some guidance from an adult helper may be necessary.

Watch points
Any concerns arising during the units which pertain to child protection issues should be referred to the designated member of staff responsible for child protection in accordance with the school's policy. Remind children they can talk to you about any issues which are raised in the activities. Reiterate that they do not have to share their work with others if they don't want to.

RoSPA
There is plenty of information on the RoSPA website (www.rospa.com) which children can assess and use to discuss safety issues in the home and the local community.

Unit 4
Am I safe?

Let's talk

Circle time and thinking activities

The question boxes provide ways to get the children thinking and talking about all the things that contribute to keeping them safe. It is important to encourage the children to take responsibility for their own safety; to discuss potential dangerous situations and people and to devise strategies for avoiding them.

1 Is it important to be safe? Should we be safe all the time? Where do you feel safe? When do you feel safe? Who do you feel safe with? What is it like to feel safe? Describe a safe feeling. Whose responsibility is our safety? Is it always the same?

2 Have you ever had an accident at home? What sort of accident was it? Could the accident have been avoided? How could it have been avoided? Are there rules at home to keep you safe? What are they designed to keep you safe from? Can you avoid all accidents?

3 Do you have a computer at home? Is it somewhere where everyone can see you using it? Why is that a good idea? What is the internet for? How do you use the internet? Do you have to think about your safety when you are on the internet?

4 Where do you play with your sports team? Are there many places to play in your community? What makes a good place to play? Where do you like to play with your friends? How do you make sure that they are safe places?

5 What are dangerous things to do? What makes them dangerous? Why shouldn't you do things which are dangerous? What might the consequences be of doing dangerous things? Are some situations dangerous? Can you describe any?

6 How do we communicate? Do we always use language – verbal or written? How else do we communicate? Do colours have meaning on the road? Why? What do they mean? Do sign shapes mean anything? (Circles are enforceable, triangles are warning.) Do pictures have a well-known meaning?

7 How many 'safe' people do you know? If you were in trouble, which people would you ask for help? Are all people 'safe'? Which people should you stay away from? (Bullies, people who ask you to do dangerous things.) What is the best strategy if you don't know someone? (Be cautious.)

8 Have you ever had to say 'no' to a friend? What did your friend want you to do? Did you know it was not a safe thing to do? Is it difficult to say 'no' to a friend? Why do you think that is?

9 When you play games, do they have rules? Why do you think there are rules? Do rules make it easier to play the game? Do rules make the game safer? Which rules can you think of which are 'safe' rules?

10 When is fire safe? When is fire not safe? What do you do in that situation? When is water safe? When is water not safe? What should you do? Is the wind sometimes safe and sometimes not safe? Can you think of examples?

Health & Wellbeing ages 9-11

Unit 4
Am I safe?

Activities

Activity 1: Staying safe

Introduce the unit by asking the children to describe what it means to 'be safe'. Brainstorm 'safe' words, write them on the whiteboard and develop a class 'safe' statement, for example, 'Feeling safe is always knowing that I am secure and protected from harm'. If appropriate, develop a class 'not safe' statement, such as 'I am not safe when I feel frightened by someone or something or I think I am in danger.'

Ask each child to write a sentence describing a 'safe' and an 'unsafe' situation, and discuss each situation with a partner. Invite the children to share their sentences and make a class list. Ask other children if they have had the same feelings or been in the same situation.

Display the **Safety web** template on the whiteboard and explain how to complete it. Arrange the children into small groups and give them copies of the template. Ask half of the class to focus on people who help keep us safe, and the other half to focus on behaviours which keep us safe. They should note all ideas, rank them and then record three or four which they believe are most important. Bring the class back together, asking each group to report their ideas and the reasons for their choices.

Extension
Encourage the children to complete their own 'safety web' and discuss it with their parents or carers.

Activity 2: Being safe at home

Begin by asking the children to think of any safety rules they have at home. These will probably not be written rules or signs, but rules their parents or carers have told them. Take feedback and make a list on the whiteboard. Do the children think that there should be safety rules at home? How do the rules help to keep them safe? Pick one of the rules listed on the whiteboard and ask a child to tell the class what accident might happen if the rule was not followed. Repeat with five or six of the rules, and invite the children to discuss the potential consequences of the remaining rules with a partner.

Give each child a copy of the core photocopiable page 64 **Risks at home**, or the support or extension version on the CD-ROM, to complete independently. Discuss their responses in class and spend some time asking for feedback on their 'How to make it safe' rules. Compile a class list of these rules.

Ask the children to discuss household emergencies in their groups, and what they would do in an emergency. Make a list of possible emergencies or accidents and ask the children to say what they would do (for example: someone gets burned in the kitchen; a young child swallows some tablets from the medicine cupboard, someone slips getting out of the bath).

Ask the children to make a list of safety devices in the home:
- smoke detectors
- fire blankets.

Activities

Unit 4

Am I safe?

Activity 3: Safe online

Use the following questions to stimulate discussion: Do you use the internet? Where do you use it? Do you chat to your friends online? How is that different to chatting on the phone? Do you prefer the phone or the internet? Is it okay to chat to people you don't know on the internet? Display the school online safety policy and discuss it with the children. Stress that it is there for their safety.

Display the **Online chat** template on the whiteboard. Arrange the children into groups and give each one of the emails from the template. Each group should discuss:
- Is it possible to tell who the email is from?
- Does the receiver know the sender? How can you tell?
- Are any of the emails a potential safety threat? How can you tell?
- Which senders would it be okay to give personal information to, or to meet?

Ask the children to write responses to the emails which they think should be responded to, but to give a strategy for dealing with the emails which should not be responded to. Check and discuss their responses, in particular any which are inappropriate.

Invite the children to suggest examples of good internet safety. As a class, agree and write a code of conduct for using the internet safely.

Activity 4: Where to play?

Set the scene by asking the children to identify 'safe' places to play locally, making a list on the whiteboard. Now ask them to identify 'unsafe' places to play in the local area. Display a large map of the area on the class wall. Give each pair of children a place from the list on the whiteboard. Ask them to make a small flag (red for unsafe and green for safe) which names the place, and then place their flags on the map.

Give each child a copy of the core photocopiable page 65 **Is it safe?** or the support or extension version on the CD-ROM, and ask them to complete it independently. When they have finished, discuss the dangers they perceived in each of the venues. Could these places be made into safe places to play? How? Invite the children to give feedback on the places they have identified as safe places to play. Stress that even safe places can become unsafe (for example, at night, or when the weather is bad, or if a person or a group who are a threat to their safety arrive). Ask them to think about how they would deal with these situations.

Extension
Encourage the children to research and write a report on an unsafe place in the community and include a digital photo of the site with their report. Display these reports in the school hall so that all children can see and read them.

Health & Wellbeing ages 9–11

Unit 4

Am I safe?

Activity 5: Danger

Set the scene by asking the children what they think of when you say the word 'danger'. In pairs, ask them to brainstorm the word and draw a mind map. Give the children just a couple of minutes for this task, and then ask for their thoughts and create a class mind map on the whiteboard.

Give each child a copy of the core photocopiable page 66 **Danger!** or the support or extension version on the CD-ROM, and ask them to complete it independently. When they have finished, recap on each situation and ensure they are all aware of the danger involved. Ask some children to share with the class what they have written about the situations. Have any of the children been in similar situations? What happened?

Arrange the children into pairs and ask them to choose a **Still life** card. Give them five minutes to develop a role play to show 'what they would do next' in their situation. Invite each pair to present their role play to the class. Ask the participants how they felt in the situation, and why they chose that resolution to the danger. Had they considered any other resolution? Ask the class whether the strategy was the best way to resolve the dangerous situation.

Develop a class list of strategies for dangerous situations, which the children could illustrate and display.

Activity 6: Road safety

Display the **Road safety signs** photos on the whiteboard. Ask the children what each sign means, and who it is aimed at. In groups, ask the children to make a collection of signs which could relate to each of these road users: pedestrians; cyclist; motorists.

Ask the children to take a couple of minutes to think about themselves as pedestrians, cyclists and motorists. Divide the class into three groups (one for each group of road users). Copy the **If, then** template and give one to each group. Within their groups the children should respond to the statements and add additional 'If, then' statements for other groups to answer. This is an open-ended activity so there should be many responses; ask the children to justify their responses.

Each road user group should then write a set of rules for their group. They could present their 'Rules for pedestrians/cyclists/motorists' to a school assembly.

It is a fact that 1.2 million people die in road accidents world-wide every year. Invite the children to work in groups to decide on a 'road safety' message which might help to save youngsters' lives. They can use the **Constructing an advertisement** template as a starting point for a poster, a radio or TV commercial. Make a school display of the 'safety messages', the advertisement plans and any final advertisements the children have time to finish.

Extension
Ask the children to design a new road safety sign, aimed particularly at themselves as road users.

Activities

Unit 4

Am I safe?

Activity 7: Safety and people

Begin the session by looking at the **Be cautious** poster from the CD-ROM. Discuss the importance of each of the rules on the poster, highlighting the safety implications and potential danger in each case.

Are there other instances when the children must be aware of their own safety when they are with people? This question will probably elicit two responses: trusted people (for example, family members or sports coaches) with whom they should be safe, but who may be inappropriate in their attentions; and bullies. It is best to give an example of the first and ask the children what they should do. Ensure they know that they can talk to you, or another member of staff, about any issues which are worrying them.

Remind the children that bullying takes many forms, and that they must keep themselves and others safe from bullies. Arrange the class in groups and ask them to brainstorm the behaviour of bullies and ways of dealing with bullies. Ask the children to plan and present a role play of a bullying scenario, with an emphasis on strategies for dealing with the bullies. Remind the children that humour is always a good weapon.

Show the interactive activity **What would a safe person do?** on the whiteboard and work through it with the class. Discuss each answer and discuss the pros and cons of each before reaching a class consensus.

Activity 8: Peer pressure

Talk with the children about the influences that other children (their peers) have on them. Children often worry that if they look 'different', nobody will like them. They often think they have to buy the trainers the others have, or that a new haircut is 'cool'. Invite the children to share their experience of a time when they were influenced by others.

Peer pressure can also affect behaviour and therefore safety. Ask the children to think of instances when peer pressure could put them in a dangerous situation. Arrange the class into small groups and ask them to discuss one of the following peer pressure situations and how their safety is compromised:
- a child offers them cigarettes, alcohol or drugs
- a child suggests they go onto the internet and look at 'fun' sites
- a child suggests they ride their bikes into the woods
- a child suggests playing in a dangerous place
- a child suggests breaking the law.

Why would someone do what a peer asks them to, even if they know it is wrong? Is it to be popular/liked? Ask the children to think about possible responses to peer pressure. Stress that it is important to make a decision and be firm, not to waver. Also, suggest that it is good to have a response ready; a funny one is always effective. Invite each group to draw a cartoon offering a response to peer pressure.

Health & Wellbeing ages 9–11

61

Unit 4
Am I safe?

Activities

Activity 9: Sports safety

Ask the children to brainstorm all the sports they know. Make a list of these on the whiteboard. Sports and games, because they are physical, have the potential to be hazardous. The most important thing is to be aware of the safety of themselves and others.

Display the interactive activity **Sports safety equipment** on the whiteboard. Discuss each of the sports in turn, and decide which piece of equipment is important for the safety of participants in that sport, and why it is necessary. Can the children think of other sports which have specialist safety equipment? Ask them to bring in any safety equipment they have from their own sports and activities to show the class.

Explain to the children that they are going to plan a summer sports gala for their school. They must decide which sports or events are going to be open to participants; where they are going to be played (this is important as they are all on the same day, although some may be staggered) and what the safety rules are going to be for each sport or event. In groups, the children choose a sport, write up the plan for that sport, the rules for participants (including safety rules) and the equipment which will be needed.

Activity 10: Fire, wind and water

Display the **Natural disasters** photos from the CD-ROM on the whiteboard and discuss each photo with the children. Make a list of the natural disasters shown in the photos. How might the people (in the photos) who live there feel? What are the consequences for them of this natural disaster? What are the safety issues which might arise in the short term, and in the longer term? (For example, issues of disease caused by stagnant water or insecure structures.)

Arrange the class into small groups and give each a copy of the **Natural disasters** template. Ask them to choose a photo and discuss it in detail, using the questions on the template as prompts. Each group should use the information generated in their group to write a report about their photo.

Tell the children to imagine they are in a place where one of these disasters occurs: a cyclone in the Caribbean, a bush fire in Australia or a tsunami in Asia. In groups, ask them to think about what they would have to do in that situation, how they would feel, how they could protect themselves and others.

Extension
Suggest that the children research a 'first aid' skill which could be useful in one of the situations outlined above. Ask them to create an easy-to-follow procedure for their classmates. Create a file of these important skills.

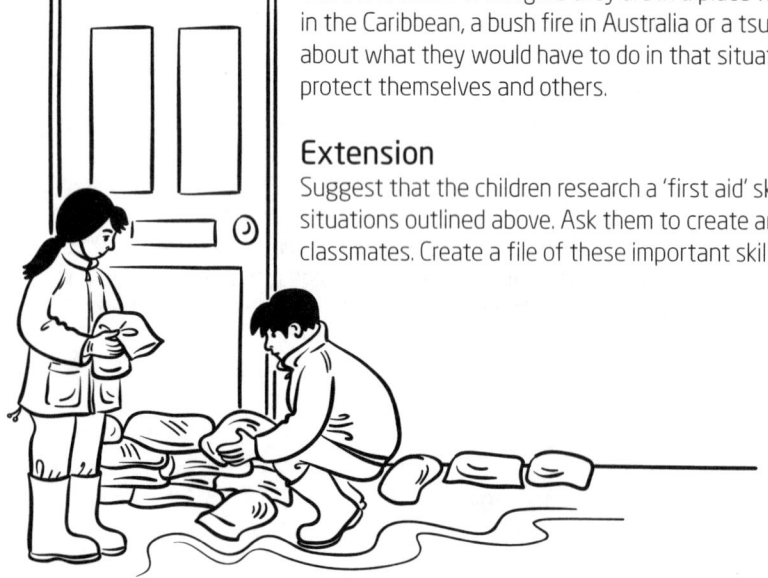

Health & Wellbeing ages **9-11**

Activities

Unit 4
Am I safe?

Activity 11: When I'm old enough

Invite the children to reflect on what they have learned during this unit. Have they learned skills which will improve their safety? Will they change any of their behaviour? Are there changes they will make in their life, at school, at home, when they are out and about? Encourage them to share their thoughts with the class.

Can the children think of safety decisions they make now, that they would not have made when they began in primary school? Ask them to brainstorm some of these decisions in pairs, and make a class list on the whiteboard. Why do they think they now make more of their own safety decisions? Is it because they are older? Lead the discussion to the concept of being more responsible.

Consider some examples of acting responsibly in a situation when safety is an issue. Can the children think of something from their own lives? If not, give them a couple to get started. Work together to complete the interactive activity **Choose your words** by adding their own speech bubbles and text, giving responsible responses. Discuss the various responses.

Display the **Safety responsibilities** template on the whiteboard and discuss each of the categories with the class. Encourage the children to think about the responsibilities they assume in their daily lives. Invite them to complete their own **Safety responsibilities** template.

Activity 12: Acting with maturity

Ask the class to reflect on the differences in how they think about safety now, compared to when they started primary school. Do they know more about potential dangers? Do they think they have a better idea about safe behaviours? Do they think they would make better decisions?

Arrange the children into groups of four or five and give each group one of the **Safety at school** cards. How would a Year 1 child deal with the situation? How would they deal with the situation? Ask them to practise two short role plays, to show the differences in behaviour. Ask them to write a statement which summarises the difference between the two attitudes.

Invite each group to perform their two role plays for the class, who must guess what the safety situation is. Does the class agree? What clues were in the role play? After the class has reviewed each role play, ask the performing group to show their statement. Does the class agree that the group has written a statement which sums up a more mature response to the situation?

Conclude by asking the children to discuss whether they have a mature attitude to their own safety. Encourage them to describe what they think that means.

Children can now complete the self-evaluation sheet or the children's booklet for the unit.

Health & Wellbeing ages **9-11**

Unit 4

Am I safe?

Photocopiable: Activity 2 | C

Risks at home

Look at each of these potential risks at home. Think about each of the dangers, then record what could happen and how it could be made safe.

Risk	What could happen?	How to make it safe
1. In the kitchen Kettle		
Knives		
Hob and oven		
2. In the bathroom Medicines		
Slippery surfaces		
Hot water		
3. In the lounge Computer		
TV		
Toys		
4. In the garden Tools		
Lawn mower		
Trees		
5. Around the house Windows and doors		
Electricity		
Cars		

My most important 'keep safe' rule at home: _____

_____

C Photocopiable: Activity 4

Unit 4

Am I safe?

Is it safe?

Look at each of the pictures. Are they safe places to play? Write down what the potential dangers are in each place.

Is it safe? Yes No
_____
_____

Is it safe? Yes No
_____
_____

Is it safe? Yes No
_____
_____

Is it safe? Yes No
_____
_____

Write about two places in your community where you like to play. Say why it is safe to play in these places.

● _____
● _____

Health & Wellbeing ages 9–11

Unit 4

Am I safe?

Photocopiable: Activity 5 | C

Danger!

Are these dangerous situations? Think about what might happen next in each of these situations and write a sentence about it.

Riding your bike along a busy road, without a helmet.
Is it dangerous? Yes / No _____

_____

Taking a tablet from a teenager you don't know.
Is it dangerous? Yes / No _____

_____

Taking shelter under a tree during an electrical storm.
Is it dangerous? Yes / No _____

_____

Going into a building site, which says 'Danger! Keep out'.
Is it dangerous? Yes / No _____

_____

Running across a busy road, dodging between the cars.
Is it dangerous? Yes / No _____

_____

Using mum or dad's password to go online.
Is it dangerous? Yes / No _____

_____

Jumping into water when you don't know how deep it is.
Is it dangerous? Yes / No _____

_____

Self-evaluation

Unit 4

Am I safe?

Keeping safe

Draw a picture of you and your friends or family being safe at home or in the community. Name the people and write a caption.

Think about the issues in this unit. Choose three that you enjoyed talking about most and say why.

- _____
- _____
- _____

Suggest other safety issues that you would like to discuss. Which issues did you discuss with your family? What did they say? _____

Which discussions and activities were the most valuable to you?

_____
_____

What do you think is the purpose of these discussions and activities? Discuss with a partner whether you think it is important to learn about safety issues in school.

_____
_____

Health & Wellbeing ages 9–11

Unit 5

Relationships

Unit planner

Aims of the unit
Children can develop a stronger sense of their own identity and place in the world around them if they have the self-confidence and self-esteem to help them form positive relationships, both within and beyond their immediate environments. Success in relationship-building will serve them well as they grow towards independence and away from the boundaries of home and school. The aim of this unit is to develop the children's understanding of many and various social interactions that they will participate in throughout their lives.

> **Key concept**
> Develop skills of interpersonal behaviour which will enable them to feel comfortable about speaking openly about opinions, values and beliefs in a supportive environment, and understand how these can be applied to national and international relations.

Learning outcomes
By the end of this unit:
- All children should be able to identify and describe the nature of the social groups of which they are part, and the responsibilities that they have for ensuring harmony within those groups. Additionally they should be beginning to realise that they sometimes need to view events from the perspective of other group members.
- Most will be able to identify and explain how to manage the dynamics of social groups, and give reasons for the concept of individual responsibility to maintain harmony within these groupings. Some may also be able to predict confidently what the consequences of their actions may be for themselves and other members of their social groups. They will be able to demonstrate respect and tolerance towards people different from themselves.
- Some may be able to discuss ways that relationships change over time, and know how to negotiate within relationships. They may demonstrate understanding and empathy towards others who live their lives in different ways and challenge prejudice and stereotyping.

Curriculum links
PSHE
- Developing good relationships and respecting the differences between people
- Preparing to play an active role as citizens

Every Child Matters
- Make a positive contribution
- Enjoy and achieve

SEAL themes
- New beginnings
- Getting on and falling out
- Say no to bullying
- Going for goals!
- Relationships

> **Vocabulary**
> Problems, changes, prejudice, persuade, unfair, respect, diversity, culture, ethnicity, racism, intolerance, gender, values, conflict, traumatic, stereotype, attitudes

Unit planner

Unit 5
Relationships

Organisation
The activities in this unit may be worked through in the order in which they appear or in another order to suit your ongoing planning. All of the activities are introduced as part of whole-class teaching. The follow-up activities include a range of individual, paired, small-group and whole-class work.

Resources
You will need the following resources to complete the activities in this unit:

Core photocopiable pages
Page 77 How to be a good friend
Page 78 All change
Page 79 Can we talk?
Page 80 Self-evaluation sheet

CD-ROM
Interactive activities:
- Aspects of bullying
- How to be fair 1
- How to be fair 2
- Respect

Photocopiables:
- How to be a good friend (support)
- How to be a good friend (extension)
- All change (support)
- All change (extension)
- Can we talk? (support)
- Can we talk? (extension)
Plus core photopiables as above

Photos:
Gender roles

Templates, cards and illustrations:
- How to beat prejudice
- Crabby Old Woman
- The gang rules!
- What bullies do
- How to be respectful
- Girls and boys
- I need to talk
- Make the right choice

Children's booklet:
Relationships

Evaluation
The self-evaluation sheet and child's booklet have been designed to allow the children to reflect upon how much they have learned about relationships during this unit. It is suggested that each child responds to the evaluation by writing, or in some cases drawing, answers according to his or her ability. Some guidance and support from an adult may be necessary at this stage.

Watch points
The nature of the material in this unit may raise sensitive issues. The activities should be undertaken in a climate of safety where children know that their opinions will be listened to and not ridiculed. Ground rules which encourage children to listen and behave sympathetically should be set, and reinforced, before, during and after the lessons. Make it clear, however, that no one is being asked to disclose anything and that the classroom is not the best place to discuss very personal problems.

Be aware of the different lifestyles and values that children learn from their homes and communities and how they might influence their opinions. There may also be some children in the class who have behavioural, social and emotional difficulties; care should be taken to ensure that they shouldn't be cited, by other children, as negative examples of ways in which to deal with the scenarios illustrated in this unit. Used sensitively, many of the activities in this unit could help these children to deal with their emotions and it could be appropriate to include some of the strategies in a behaviour improvement plan.

Unit 5
Relationships

Let's talk

Circle time and thinking activities

The question boxes provide ways to get the children thinking and talking about the factors that contribute to making them who they are. It is important to encourage the children not simply to think about their body image, but to focus instead on their personal qualities and values.

1 Are all of us exactly the same? In what ways are we different? In what ways are we alike? Are differences bad? Why/Why not? Are some children picked on because they are different? How are they picked on? How might they feel about this? How do you feel about it?

2 What is prejudice? How is prejudice different from not liking someone? Can you think of different forms of prejudice? Have you ever experienced prejudice? In what way? How did it make you feel? How do prejudiced people treat others? How do people become prejudiced?

3 Do you know any elderly people? How old are people before they can be described as 'elderly'? What happens to adults as they get older? Can elderly people help you? How? What can you learn from old people? Are there any advantages to being elderly?

4 Why are friendships so important to us? What makes a good friend? Is there such a thing as a bad friend? Do best friends always have to do everything together? What should friendship be based on? Do best friends always have to agree with each other?

5 What is a bully? Why might someone be bullied? Why is bullying wrong? If you are the victim of bullying, what should you do? Why do people bully others? Can someone be a bully without meaning to be? How can we persuade people not to bully others?

6 Have you ever said, 'That's unfair'? When? How do you know when something is unfair? What does treating people 'fairly' mean? Is it possible to be fair to everyone? Should you try? Why/Why not? Are all people in Britain treated fairly? Are there any laws concerning fair treatment for all?

7 In what ways do you treat people with respect? Are there ways in which you don't? How can we respect our homes, neighbourhoods and schools? Do you know of any disrespectful behaviour? How do you feel about it? Are we all entitled to respect or do we have to earn it?

8 Do you have a different best friend than a year ago? Why? How might a child react to a new brother or sister? What are the best and worst things about having a new teacher? How have you dealt with changes in the past? How will you deal with future changes?

9 Should girls and boys play different games? Should men and women follow different occupations? Are boys stronger than girls? Do girls cry more easily than boys? Who should earn more, men or women? What do you like or dislike about being a girl/boy?

10 Should all secrets be kept? Could you cause harm to another person or yourself by keeping a secret? Who might you share a 'worrying' secret with? What is the difference between keeping a secret because you want to, or keeping a secret because someone else has told you to?

Unit 5
Relationships

Activities

Activity 1: Tolerance

Start by quoting from the Queen's Christmas message of 2002, when she spoke of her sense of sharing a common heritage '...enriched by the cultural, ethnic and religious diversity of our 21st century society'. Ask the children what they think the Queen meant.

Continue by reminding the children that people are not only different because of culture or ethnicity. Ask them to identify other differences. Ensure that they include differences of age, of talents and aptitudes, of strengths and of weaknesses. Explain that we tend mainly to celebrate those who are like ourselves; who are of a similar age, have similar interests, share the same aptitudes. We might dislike or distrust people who are different from us.

Identify and discuss examples of historical group hatred or distrust (for example, religious persecution, witch hunts, Elizabeth 1 and the Blackamoors). Ask the children to suggest similar current examples: racism, religious intolerance, gender issues and so on. Be sensitive to the feelings and experiences of your class and take care to avoid highlighting examples of intolerance which might instigate such behaviours.

Discuss reasons why some people dislike a whole group, without even knowing them. Elicit responses such as fear, threat, rumours, myths and so on.

Ask the children to identify any school rules which discourage intolerance. Do they think that the school's values are reflected in the wider community? Why/Why not? How do they think they can promote tolerance at home, and in their local neighbourhood?

Activity 2: Prejudice

Display the **How to beat prejudice** poster from the CD-ROM. Discuss each point and ask for illustrative examples. Discuss with the children how the following situations may, or may not, be showing prejudice: making fun of someone's physical appearance; leaving someone out of a team because he can't run fast; teasing people because they speak with a strong accent; ignoring someone because she uses a wheelchair; not letting someone play with trains because she's a girl; not letting someone take ballet lessons because he is a boy.

Arrange the children into groups and ask them to role play the following situation. Some good friends are planning to spend a day at the local leisure centre. Two of them want to invite another child who's new to the school. The others don't want to include this person because he/she is different in some way (for example, they are from a different culture, they wear glasses). After the role play have a class discussion about the arguments for and against inviting the newcomer.

Suggest the children perform another role play in their groups, changing what is different about the newcomer. How have their responses changed? Which issues have both role plays got in common?

Work with the class to make a list of words which describe how people feel when they are left out. Make another list of words which describe how people feel when they are asked to join in an activity. Invite the children to use the lists to help them write a poem or story about a time when they felt they had been left out.

Unit 5

Relationships

Activity 3: Old age

Display and discuss the poem **Crabby Old Woman** from the CD-ROM. It is a moving poem that deals with the feelings of an elderly lady as she looks back at her life, and requires a mature and sensitive approach from the children. Explain that the poem was found in the possessions of an old lady who had died in hospital. Encourage the children to consider the writer's feelings, and how she describes each stage of her life. Organise the class into groups and allocate each group a few verses to incorporate into a class PowerPoint presentation of the complete poem.

Ask the children to think of a situation when an older person appeared not to understand them and perhaps created a conflict or difficulty. Encourage them to think about what led to the misunderstanding and what happened as a result. Help them to see the situation through the elderly person's eyes. What might the children do in the future to avoid a similar misunderstanding?

Ask the children to role play the following scenario in their groups. An old-age pensioner, whose health is not very good, needs a lot of sleep and goes to bed early. During the light summer evenings he is often disturbed by a group of young neighbours hanging around outside his house laughing, talking and playing music. He tries to explain his needs to the youngsters.

Extension

Invite a representative of Age Concern to visit the school and talk to your class. Consider befriending a group of elderly people in the school neighbourhood. Invite them to school events, assemblies, and so on. Think of ways in which the children can help them throughout the year.

Activity 4: The best of friends or the worst of friends?

Set the scene by saying that the children are to imagine that they've been invited to join a gang of older children. They are really pleased because it makes them feel grown up, but they are being asked to do things that they feel is wrong. Do they go along with the gang's wishes?

Organise the children into groups and give each one a scenario from **The gang rules!** cards. Ask each group to consider their situation. How would they feel in that position? What would they do? During a plenary session, the groups should describe their scenarios and their reactions to it. If appropriate, some of the groups could present their findings as a role play.

Ask the children if they think that such gang members are really good friends. How would they define a good friend? Write the statement 'To have good friends, you must be a good friend!' on the whiteboard. Ask the children to explain what the statement might mean, and to tell you why they either agree or disagree with it.

Ask the children to think of ways that good friends treat each other. List their answers on the whiteboard and discuss each one. Hand out the core photocopiable page 77 **How to be a good friend**, or the support or extension version on the CD-ROM, for them to complete independently.

Activities

Unit 5

Relationships

Activity 5: Bullying/cruelty

Tell the beginning of the story of Joseph from Genesis, or remind the children of the plot of the musical version. Joseph was the second youngest of twelve sons, and favoured by his father, who gave him a multicoloured coat. His brothers became very jealous of him and hatched a plot to get rid of him – they ripped up his coat, threw him in a deep pit and eventually sold him into slavery, telling their father that he had been killed. Only one of the brothers, Reuben, tried to save Joseph. Why were Joseph's brothers unkind to him? Do they think that the plot to kill Joseph was bullying that got out of hand? Discuss Reuben's role. Did he do his best or could he have done more to help Joseph?

Brainstorm ways in which people can be bullied. Organise the children into groups and give each one three cards from the **What bullies do** template. Encourage the groups to discuss their experiences of each scenario. Although they may have personal experiences, some children will feel more comfortable relating the situations to a television programme, film or story. Traditional fairytales are often a good starting point.

After the small-group discussions, invite feedback. Brainstorm ideas for dealing with each of the different bullying tactics. Use the interactive activity **Aspects of bullying**, working with the children to drag and drop each answer to the appropriate question. Challenge the children to add further answers to some of the questions.

Explain that sometimes it is difficult to know what is, or is not, bullying. Often, actions start out as fun, but can turn into bullying. Write the 'Am I a bully?' questions on the whiteboard. If the children are not sure if the way they have been treating someone has become bullying they should stop, think and ask themselves the questions.

Activity 6: Fairness

Ask the children to think about how many times in their lives they have said 'It's not fair!'. Discuss the kinds of occasions when they say 'It's not fair!' Explain that young children learn simple lessons about fairness when they have to take turns when playing a game, or share treats equally. As we grow we begin to understand that fairness involves more than these simple ideas.

Brainstorm a list of rules for being fair and ask for specific examples of 'fair behaviour' for each. Use the interactive activities **How to be fair 1 & 2** to reinforce rules of fairness and introduce new ones. Help the children to understand some of the more complex rules by discussing them more fully. For example, ask them what is meant by 'taking unfair advantage'. Illustrate this by reminding the children of the story of the Little Red Hen. Ask them if it was fair that the other animals expected to take advantage of the Little Red Hen's hard work.

When they have understood this simple example, ask the children to think of and describe a time when they've taken unfair advantage of a person or a situation, or when someone has taken unfair advantage of them. Did they learn anything from the experience?

Challenge the children to give examples of things that happen in the world that seem to be unfair. What could be done to rectify these injustices? Whose responsibility is it? How could we contribute to the effort?

Unit 5
Relationships

Activity 7: Respect!

Ask the children what they think of when they hear the word 'Respect'. They might mention Ali G and Hip Hop culture. If they do, explain that this culture arose from a call for respect from impoverished and marginalised sections of American society.

Discuss the ways in which we show people respect. These could include being kind, sharing, being friendly and so on, especially to people who we think don't have much in common with us.

Ensure that the children understand that respect is not only about the deference you show to people in authority. Respect is about recognising the worth of every human being, even those who have no power over you. Illustrate this by working with the children to complete the interactive activity **Respect**.

Brainstorm some guidelines for respect with the class. When they have exhausted their ideas, compare their list with the **How to be respectful** poster from the CD-ROM. Go through each item on the poster and ask the children to describe ways in which we could be disrespectful by doing the opposite of what is suggested. Then ask how those actions could be changed to become more respectful.

Work with the children to develop a 'Respect contract' which embodies a set of rules for having a respectful classroom. Display the contract in the classroom and refer to it whenever a reminder is needed.

Activity 8: Life changes and challenges

Introduce the activity by asking the children to suggest events which cause people to make changes in their lifestyle. Ideas might include moving house, moving school, death and divorce. Make a list of these suggestions on the whiteboard and ask the children to rank them in order in terms of the most traumatic to the least traumatic. Encourage them to talk about their reasons for this ranking.

Explain that, after death and divorce, the third most traumatic event in an adult's life is moving house. Where was that event in their list? Why is it such a traumatic change for adults? Although a house move is traumatic for the adults in the family, it could involve another traumatic change for young people – moving school. Ask the children what would worry them most about moving school. List their responses on the whiteboard and discuss. Emphasise the differences between moving to secondary school where the whole year group is new, and being the only new child in a school.

Discuss the changes that have happened in the children's lives throughout primary school. Give each child a copy of the core photocopiable page 78 **All change**, or the support or extension version on the CD-ROM, to complete independently. After completion, organise the children into small groups and invite them to share their findings.

Ask the children to suggest ways in which they could welcome a new child to their class in order to help them overcome their fears and worries. Incorporate their ideas into a class charter for welcoming new children.

Children can now complete the self-evaluation sheet or the children's booklet for the unit.

Activities

Unit 5

Relationships

Activity 9: Boy meets girl

Show and distribute the **Girls and boys** template from the CD-ROM. Ask the children to think very carefully about what they like and dislike about each gender, and enter their opinions in each quarter. Take feedback and discuss the merits and problems associated with each suggestion. (Be prepared for this to be a very lively session!) Introduce the notion that not everyone conforms to a gender stereotype.

Display the **Gender roles** photos from the CD-ROM on the whiteboard. Ask the children to discuss each picture and whether or not the roles depicted could, or should, be undertaken by persons of the opposite gender. Talk to the class about roles traditionally thought about as being particularly suitable for boys or girls. During a plenary session, discuss if stereotyping people by gender is a serious issue. What, if anything, can be done about it?

Subsequent discussions should lead to the children's reflections on how they relate to people of both genders. Would they prefer male or female teachers? Do they get on better with male or female carers? Have they got both male and female friends? Which do they prefer? Are the answers given by the boys and girls always the same, or are there differences?

Ask the class if they think that their answers might change as they get older. If so, which ones and why? (Use your knowledge of the individuals in your class to make sensitive judgements about discussing issues of sexual attraction and orientation.)

Conclude that feelings and attitudes to the opposite sex change and develop at different rates. All are normal but none are typical.

Activity 10: Secrets

Ask the children to suggest some situations in which they would need to tell another person who they trusted about something that was worrying them, such as moving school, bullying, parents arguing, approaching puberty.

Who could they talk to? Make sure that the children understand that you are asking for roles, not names (for example, 'a teacher' not 'Ms Mead'). What kind of person would they confide in? Explain to the children that it is often easy to think of who to talk to, but finding the right words might be difficult. What else might get in the way of confiding in someone? Ensure that they include finding the right moment, lack of privacy, plucking up courage, thinking they'll get into trouble, being embarrassed and being frightened that they'll be laughed at. Give each child a copy of the core photocopiable page 79 **Can we talk?** or the support or extension version on the CD-ROM, to complete independently. Provide an opportunity for the children to discuss their completed sheet with you, if they wish.

Organise the children into pairs and give each a scenario from the **I need to talk** cards. Ask them to read each situation carefully and prepare a short role play illustrating the way in which they can approach someone and begin to discuss a problem. Emphasise that they don't need to solve the problem on their cards, but show ways in which a conversation might be started.

Remind the children that although telling a trusted person about a problem may be difficult, keeping quiet can be even worse. Research and discuss the range of professional or voluntary sources of help that can be accessed free of charge.

Health & **Wellbeing** ages **9-11**

Unit 5
Relationships

Activity 11: Relationships between nations/societies

Ask the children what they have learned during this unit. Consider how the lessons might also be useful for leaders of communities and countries. Investigate how the values identified in the unit apply to the local community.

Continue by considering issues related to the wider world. Discuss the concept of fairness as it applies to world poverty. Is it fair that the world is divided into rich and poor nations? How could we make our world a fairer world? Should we send aid to other countries, and how should this be used? Talk about Live Aid, Comic Relief, Sports Aid and other fundraising initiatives.

Extend these ideas by asking if we should pay higher prices for commodities imported from the Third World. Discuss fair trade and research any fair trade products that are available locally.

Consider how the idea of respect can be extended to respect for the environment. Discuss pollution of water and air, noise levels, litter, graffiti and so on. Does this show respect for our world?

Refer either to current conflicts, or conflicts that occurred during the period of history that the children are studying or have previously studied. Explain that wars, like quarrels between children, usually begin because of intolerance, prejudice, greed, envy, bullying or other unkind acts.

Conclude by asking the children to adapt some of the rules learnt in the *Tolerance, Prejudice, Bullying/cruelty, Fairness* and *Respect!* activities to apply to relationships between nations.

Activity 12: Deciding what's right

Divide the class into small groups. Give each group a scenario from the **Make the right choice** cards. Ask the groups to divide in two to role play their situation; half the group should do the wrong thing and the other half should do the right thing. Each must give strong reasons for their actions. Discuss the results in a class plenary.

Ask the children if they have ever really wanted to do something, but deep down felt it wasn't right. How did they decide what to do? Who or what influenced their decision? Why do people sometimes do the right thing, even when it's not as easy or as much fun as the alternative? How do you know when something is the right or wrong thing to do? Brainstorm ways to tell whether or not something is the right thing to do, listing ideas on the whiteboard. Write the 'How do I decide what's right?' list on the whiteboard and compare with the children's ideas.

Extend the idea to focus on choices the children might make to improve the world we live in. Would they choose to make more roads to cope with increasing car ownership, or improve the public transport system? Would they hand out tougher sentences to criminals, or try to stop people breaking the law in the first place? Use other current national and international issues to lead the children to discuss what choices they would make.

Children can now complete the self-evaluation sheet or the children's booklet for the unit.

C Photocopiable: Activity 4

Unit 5

Relationships

How to be a good friend

Here are some rules for being good friends. Think about some times when you followed each rule and write what happened.

Good friends always listen to each other.	Good friends don't put each other down or hurt each other's feelings.
Good friends try to understand each other's feelings and moods.	Good friends help each other to solve problems.
Good friends give each other compliments.	Good friends can disagree without hurting each other.

Health & Wellbeing ages 9-11

Unit 5

Photocopiable: Activity 8 C

Relationships

All change

Think about changes that have taken place in your life since you were in Year 1.

1. Who did you play with when you were in Year 1?
   _____.

2. Who are your friends now?
   _____.

3. Who has been your friend for the longest time?
   _____.

4. Have any changes happened in your family since you were in Year 1?
   _____.

5. Have any changes happened in your school since you were in Year 1?
   _____.

6. How have you changed since you were in Year 1?
   _____.

7. Which changes since you were in Year 1 have made you happy?
   _____.

8. Which changes since you were in Year 1 have made you unhappy?
   _____.

9. What changes are you looking forward to in the next few years?
   _____.

10. Which changes might be most challenging?
    _____.

C Photocopiable: Activity 10

Unit 5

Relationships

Can we talk?

Think about who you can talk to when you have a problem. Use a rating of 1 to 3 to show how easy or difficult it would be to talk about each topic with your parents, teachers or friends.

Ratings 1 = Easy 2 = Quite easy 3 = Quite difficult 4 = Very difficult

Problem	Parents	Teachers	Friends
Someone has asked you to go to bowling with them, but you don't know if you should.			
You don't think you are going to do very well in your tests.			
You think your mum is always too busy to take any notice of you.			
You help a lot around the house, but your younger brother never does.			
Your friends always promise to come and play with you at the weekend, but they never do.			
A boy in your class has stopped speaking to you, and you don't know why.			
Your dad won't let you stay at after-school club, but you don't know his reasons.			
Your two best friends have recently started smoking. They want you to join them, and are teasing you because you won't.			
It is Friday and you have just been given a large amount of homework, which is to be handed in on Monday. Your parents have arranged to take you to visit relatives at the weekend.			

Write a list of other people you could talk to if you had a problem.

_____

Who do you usually find it most easy to talk to? _____

Why?_____

Health & Wellbeing ages 9-11   Photocopiable   **SCHOLASTIC** 79
www.scholastic.co.uk

Unit 5

Relationships

Self-evaluation

Relationships

Name _____

Before you complete this sheet, think carefully about all of the activities you have done in this unit. Look at the displays in the classroom and check back on some of the work in your books and folders.

I have learned more about _____

_____

I would still like to learn more about _____

_____

I enjoyed _____

because _____

I did not really enjoy _____

because _____

_____

I did best when _____

I think I need more help when _____

_____

_____

The most important thing I learned about my relationships was _____

_____

_____

_____

_____

Unit 6

My community and environment

Unit planner

Aims of the unit
Children can develop a strong sense of themselves as members of communities and appreciate that there are differences and similarities between members of communities. They understand that being an active member of a community (or communities) is a benefit to themselves and to the community in which they live, and that their actions affect themselves and others in the community. As they approach the final years of their primary schooling they make more decisions independently, and have an appreciation of the importance of looking after their community and the environment. Looking after our community and the environment is important to us all.

> **Key concept**
> Develop an increasing understanding of belonging to a community, and the concepts of roles and responsibilities in a community and the environment in which it exists.

Learning outcomes
By the end of this unit:
- All children should be able to explain why it is important to make choices about their community and environment; they can identify potential risks to them and understand what they can do to reduce these potential risks. They can also understand community needs, their benefits and the responsibilities of membership.
- Most will be able to understand how they can influence change, and identify how their actions and the actions of others have consequences for their communities and the environment.
- Some may be able to reflect on and evaluate their actions, and those of others, to maintain good relationships within their community and respond to, or challenge negative behaviours in others. They will be able to demonstrate effective ways of resisting external pressures, including negative pressure from their peers, and show a concern for their environment.

Curriculum links
PSHE
- Preparing to play a role as active citizens
- Developing confidence and responsibility and making the most of their abilities
- Developing good relationships and respecting the differences between people

Every Child Matters
- Make a positive contribution
- Enjoy and achieve

SEAL themes
- Changes
- Relationships

Literacy
- Presenting an argument
- Writing arguments 'for' and 'against' an issue
- Reviewing the features of newspaper reports

ICT
- Preparing a PowerPoint presentation

> **Vocabulary**
> Community, environment, needs, wants, transport, leisure, entertainment, utilities, services, rules, laws, disability, law makers, law breakers, conventional, unconventional, vandalism, pollution, graffiti, rubbish, fumes, protection, endangered, rights, equality, justice, necessity, luxury, responsibility, poverty, peace, universal

Unit 6

My community and environment

Unit planner

Organisation
The activities in this unit may be worked through in the order in which they appear or in another order to suit your ongoing planning. All of the activities are introduced as part of whole-class teaching. The follow-up activities include a range of individual, paired, small-group and whole-class work.

Resources
You will need the following resources to complete the activities in this unit:

Core photocopiable pages
Page 90 Needs and wants – a different perspective
Page 91 Survey of facilities for disabled people
Page 92 Cheating
Page 93 Self-evaluation sheet

CD-ROM
Interactive activities:
- Needs and wants
- The law
- Breaking the law

Photocopiables:
- Needs and wants – a different perspective (support)
- Needs and wants – a different perspective (extension)
- Cheating (support)
- Cheating (extension)

Plus core photopiables as above
Photos:
Necessity or luxury

Templates, cards and illustrations:
- Different children
- Have your say
- Courtroom drama
- Vandalism
- Do's and don't's
- Rights of the child
- Who does what?
- Issue analysis
- My view
- Making a positive contribution
- Rights and responsibilities
- Arguments
- Reflection

Children's booklet:
My community and environment

Evaluation
The self-evaluation sheet and children's booklet have been designed to allow the children to assess how much they have learned about keeping healthy during this unit. It is suggested that the child responds to the evaluation by writing, or in some cases drawing, answers according to his or her ability. Some guidance from an adult helper may be necessary.

Watch points
Be aware of the different communities in the class, particularly religious communities, and ensure that discussion of these communities is approached sensitively and without bias. Encourage all the children to express themselves during the activities, and place adult help in group activities where a child or children may have difficulty. Some activities may require adaptation to suit a range of individual needs and learning styles, to ensure that all children respond according to their abilities.

Unit 6

My community and environment

Let's talk

Circle time and thinking activities

The question boxes provide ways to get the children thinking and talking about the communities they live in and the environment we all share. It is important to encourage the children not simply to think about their immediate community and environment, but to think more broadly about the communities around them, and the environment in a national and international sense.

1 What does the word 'community' mean? What makes a community? Are communities different? How many communities do you belong to? Are they different/the same? How? Who do we share each community with? Which communities do we stay in all our lives? Which new ones do we belong to?

2 What are the things all people need? Are the needs of people different, depending on their age? Are needs different depending on where you live? Why are needs sometimes different? What do you want? Do you want things, people, and experiences? Do we all want the same things?

3 How do communities meet the needs of their members? What are the needs of the school community? How are these met? Does the swimming club meet the same needs as the school? Which community provides you with shelter and food?

4 Do you think it is important that rules are fair? What does 'fair' mean? Can you give some examples of rules at school which are fair? Are there any rules at school which you think are not fair? Why? How could they be made fair?

5 Why do we have laws in our community? Who makes the laws? Which laws do you know? Who are they for? Do you try to obey the laws? What would happen if you didn't obey the laws? Is it important to have laws in a community?

6 Do all laws apply to children? Should all laws apply to children? How many laws do you know which apply just to children? (Road safety.) Why do these laws apply to children? Are they for your protection? Do you obey these laws? Should you obey the laws? Why? Why not?

7 Have you heard of the 'rights of the child'? What do you think it might be? Is it important for children to have rights? Should all children have the same rights? Do you think your parents (and grandparents) had the same rights as you? How are they different?

8 How do you use water each day? (Cooking, drinking and staying clean.) How much water do you use every day? Have you ever been without water – when the mains burst, or you are camping? Were you pleased to have it back? How could you stop wasting water?

9 What do you think are the most important environmental issues in the world? Why? Are there any environmental issues where you live? What are they? Why are they important to you and to the community? Can you help? Can your family help? Who else can help?

10 Do you read the newspaper, listen to the radio or watch TV? Do you get information about the world from these media? Do you believe what you read or see? Why/Why not? Is it important to think about what you read and see and make your own decisions?

No running in the corridors. Speed cameras operate in this school.

Unit 6

My community and environment

Activities

Activity 1: My community

Start by asking the children how many communities they belong to. Suggest they start by thinking of the community closest to them (their family), and then moving out from there. They could make a diagrammatic representation of the different communities.

Organise the children into groups of four or five, and give each a scenario from the **Different children** cards. Ask each group to discuss the child they have been given, and the communities and groups to which they belong. Ask them to consider whether the children belong to the groups because they have chosen to belong, or because they have been born into them. Encourage them to consider the benefits of belonging to each group and how they contribute to each group. Write a table with these headings on the whiteboard and ask each group to complete the table for the communities and groups their child belongs to:

| Community | How it helps them | How they help it |

When the children have completed their tables, ask each group to give feedback to the class. What is special about each community/group? How do we know that people belong to groups? (Team scarves, badges and other outward signs.) Reinforce the importance of accepting the differences in people who belong to different communities.

Ask the children to complete the table for their own communities independently, adding a column 'Why I belong'. When they have completed their own table, they can share it with a partner. Make a class display of all the communities in your class.

Extension
Encourage the children to make a list of the communities or groups they might belong to in the future, particularly in secondary school. Suggest that they research the clubs and groups.

Activity 2: Needs and wants

Explain that different people have different needs and wants. Brainstorm ideas as to why people might have different needs and wants, for example, age, body type (disabled or able-bodied), where you live. Arrange the children into small groups and ask them to agree the four most important needs of a baby and an older person. Ensure they have focused on needs, not wants.

Explain that there are some things that we all need. Display the interactive activity **Needs and wants** on the whiteboard. As you work through the activity, ask the children their reasons for placing statements in their respective places. At the end of the activity agree a class definition of 'need' – those things which are important for a happy and healthy life, many of which they cannot provide for themselves; and 'wants' – those things that they would like to have. At the end of the activity, ask the children to work with a partner to place their 'needs' statements in order from the most important to the least important.

Provide each child with a copy of the core photocopiable page 90 **Needs and wants – a different perspective**, or the support or extension version on the CD-ROM, to complete independently. Invite children to give feedback to the class, although be sensitive to their different circumstances. Discuss why the needs and wants of a child in the developing world might be different to their own. Introduce the 'Rights of the Child' concept and discuss their thoughts. Suggest they look at the website www.therightssite.org.uk. This will be discussed in more detail in Activity 7.

Activities

Unit 6

My community and environment

Activity 3: Meeting community needs

Consider how communities try to meet the needs of all their members, even though some of their needs are different. Ask the children to think of their needs which are met by the wider community (for example, education, transport, leisure).

Work with the class to record other groups in the community who have different needs. Organise the children into small groups and give each one of the following groups: older people; people with disabilities; children under five. Ask them to make a list of needs for the group and then how each need is, or could be, met. Ask each group to feed back to the class. How do they rate the way the community meets the needs of their group on a scale of 1–5?

Ask the children about any disabled people they know. Are there any children in the school with disabilities? If someone in the class has a disability, ascertain before the lesson if they are happy to answer questions about their disabilities. If not, explain that the person does not want to talk about it now. Do they understand the needs of disabled people in their community? Make a list of things they think the community should provide for disabled people. Provide the class with a copy of the school access policy and discuss its relevance to disabled pupils and visitors.

Initiate a discussion of venues in the community which all people want to visit, including those with disabilities (theatres, cinemas, council offices, police stations and so on). Arrange visits to various venues and conduct a survey using photocopiable page 91 **Survey of facilities for disabled people**. After the visits, ask groups to share their findings with the class and decide if any follow-up is required, such as a letter to the Council or the local newspaper.

Activity 4: Rules at school

Ask the children to tell you what school rules they know and make an initial list on the whiteboard. Consider who might have made each rule, e.g. government (health and safety legislation); school management (rules about bullying, cheating); school council (recycling).

Ask each child to choose one rule from any group and prepare a 30–45 second resume for the class. They should include information about the rule, where it comes from, whether it is fair or not and whether it could/should be improved or changed. Keep a record of suggested changes or improvements. At the end of the session, ask the children what they would like to do: hold a class council to discuss such matters; take the issues to the school council? Provide copies of the **Have your say** template and invite them to add their comments. Discuss the findings with the class, and move to action the majority view.

Think of some examples of breaking a school rule, such as smoking at school or bullying. Ask the class what they would do if they saw someone breaking a school rule. Discuss each strategy suggested by the children and agree on a definitive list. Ask: *Is cheating against school rules? Is it right or wrong?* Give pairs of children a copy of the core photocopiable page 92 **Cheating**, or the support or extension version on the CD-ROM, and ask them to discuss what they would do in each situation. Discuss their responses. Why could some children be tempted to cheat? What is the alternative?

Extension
How effective is your school council? Children can go to the website www.schoolcouncils.org, download a copy of the 'How are we doing?' template and run a school survey. They can then suggest future changes and improvements.

Health & Wellbeing ages 9–11

Unit 6

My community and environment

Activity 5: Respect the law

Ask the class to imagine what it would be like living in a place with no laws, where people could do what they liked. What would happen? Would they like to live in a lawless society? Would some groups be particularly vulnerable? Why?

Display the interactive activity **The law** on the whiteboard. Read out each statement asking the children to discuss each briefly with a partner and justify their responses. Discuss individual views before reaching a class consensus for each statement. How would they find out more?

Arrange the class into small groups and ask them to make a list of laws they know which fit into these categories: laws for the roads; laws about property (personal and community); laws which protect people; laws about how we treat other people.

Arrange the class into groups of six and provide each with one of the scenarios from the **Courtroom drama** cards. Explain that the children will first need to allocate the six roles. Give them some time to think about their roles and what they will say (particularly the witness, who must decide which pupil he or she is going to support). Allow the group to practise and then perform their role play for the class, who will act as the jury. At the end of the role play the judge should ask the 'jury' for a vote.

Activity 6: Children and the law

Display the **Vandalism** illustrations on the whiteboard, and ask the children what they see in each illustration in turn. Why are the children doing what they are doing? Will anyone suffer because of their actions? Are they breaking the law? What are the possible consequences?

Discuss with the class the list of laws you made in Activity 5: laws for the roads; laws about property (personal and community); laws which protect people; laws about how we treat other people. Do these laws relate to children? Make a class list of questions the children have about themselves and the law. Ask a member of the local police force to come to school and talk to the children about the law and them, focusing particularly on laws which particularly apply to children. Create a 'Children and the law' display. Group the laws into categories (as above) and include comments and illustrations from the children.

Display the interactive activity **Breaking the law** on the whiteboard and discuss the first scenario. Complete the activity, giving the children time to discuss each scenario with a partner first. When the activity has been completed, discuss how to make sure you don't break the law, and the consequences of following others. Make a class list of strategies to stay within the law.

Give each child a copy of the **Do's and don't's** template to complete independently. Suggest that they share their work with their families or their friends.

Activities

Unit 6

My community and environment

Activity 7: Rights of the child

Display the **Rights of the child** poster from the CD-ROM. Discuss the three articles with the class. Explain to the children that this Convention of Rights (which is almost 20 years old) has been ratified by all the countries of the world, except Somalia and the USA. They are the first generation to have grown up with such protection.

Refer back to the work done on 'needs and wants' in Activity 2. Ask the children what they think 'rights' are. Are 'rights' about needs or wants? What rights do children think are important? Responses could include: 'a house to live in'; 'protection from harm'. Make a list of all the suggestions on the whiteboard. Display the 'child friendly' UN Convention on the Rights of the Child from www.therightssite.org.uk on the whiteboard. How many of the children's suggestions are mentioned? Choose some of the articles for discussion – for example, Articles 8, 12, 13, 19, 23, 24 and 28. Why do the children think the Convention is important? Are some of these rights more difficult to obtain in some countries than in others?

Write these headings on the whiteboard: 'The right to live'; 'The right to be cared for'; 'The right to be protected'; 'The right to have a say'; 'The right to learn and play'. Arrange the class into groups and ask each group to focus on one of the headings. They should then look through the Convention and add 5 or 6 Articles which they think are described by their heading. For example 'The right to live and grow' might include Articles 6, 23, 24 and 26.

Conclude by asking the children to consider if all children have these rights. If not, what can be done, by them or by others? You will find useful statistics about child labour and exploitation on the UNICEF website www.unicef.org.uk.

Activity 8: A wider world

Remind the children of the work they did in Activity 2 on 'needs and wants' and the work on 'rights' in Activity 7. Remind them of the differences between their own lives and the lives of children in the wider world. Organise the class into groups and ask them to brainstorm problematic issues for children living in Africa, South America or some parts of Asia – for example, war, global warming, climate change, famine, exploitation of children as workers. Make a class list of these issues.

Display the **Necessity or luxury** photos from the CD-ROM on the whiteboard. As you look at each image, ask the children if they consider it a necessity or a luxury. Discuss their responses and take a straw poll. Introduce the idea that while some of the images may be 'necessities' for children in Britain and the west, they are in fact a luxury for children in other parts of the world (for example, washing fruit and vegetables, or having a shower).

Work with the class to decide on some other important issues from the wider world. Ask the children, in groups, to choose one of these issues and research it together. Suggest that they use the **Who does what?** template, to assign tasks to each group member. The children could begin their research by completing the **Issue analysis** template. Encourage them to make a display of their research, and to complete the task by making a group statement. If possible, ask the children to peer-review each others' work.

Health & Wellbeing ages 9-11

Unit 6

My community and environment

Activity 9: Environmental issues

Review the issues for the wider world you discussed in Activity 8. Did you discuss global warming, problems with the ozone layer, waste disposal via landfill, transport and endangered species? Tell the children that today you are going to focus on animals which are endangered because their environment is threatened. Do they know any animals in this category?

Show the children a video showing polar bears in their habitat and how it is changing (for example, BBC series *The Blue Planet;* National Geographic *On Thin Ice*). Before screening, ask the children to write a list of questions they want to find out; see if they can find answers during the video.

In pairs, ask the children to choose an animal environment and research what is happening to it. What, if anything can be done to save the environment? Display the **My view** template and talk to the class about how to present an argument. Suggest that they use the template for their presentation; they do not have to write a lot, but should include key sentences and possibly drawings which will help them to remember their main points.

> Where do polar bears live?
>
> What is important about their habitat?
>
> How have they adapted to their habitat?
>
> Has something changed in their habitat?

Extension

The children can follow up their 'arguments' by deciding on one thing which they could do which might help. Suggest that they commit to undertaking this one thing in the next two weeks (if possible). Review progress after an appropriate time.

Activity 10: Environment and the media

Collect a range of newspapers, all reporting the same environmental issue. If possible, scan these and display them one by one on the interactive whiteboard. Discuss each one with the class and use the whiteboard tools to highlight and draw attention to the following:
- The headline
- The introductory sentence
- Statistics quoted, or alluded to
- Sources quoted, or alluded to
- Use of emotive language
- Use of exaggeration

Ask the children, in groups, to compare two or three of the reports. For example, are the statistics the same in each report? Why are they not the same? Is this misleading? Can they rely on the quoted source (or sources)? How does the use of language alter the report? Ask each group to provide feedback on their findings to the class. Encourage them to talk about what they have learned about newspaper reporting. Does this affect how they regard media reports?

Extension

Keep copies of some local newspaper articles which deal with environmental issues. Ask someone from your local newspaper to come to your school and talk about the reporting of these stories in their newspaper.

Activities

Unit 6
My community and environment

Activity 11: Making a positive contribution

Throughout the unit the children have been learning more about their communities, and the rights and responsibilities of themselves and of others. Has this given them a stronger sense of the things that they 'believe in', be it at school or elsewhere? Ask them all to take a few minutes to make a list of 'the things that they believe in'. Ask some of the children to share the things they believe in with the class, and discuss how they can do something about these issues.

Give pairs of children a copy of the **Making a positive contribution** template. Encourage them to use it to record the things they believe in, and how they can make a positive contribution. When they have had time to consider all areas, ask for feedback from the class.

Invite each pair to choose the most important of the things they believe in, to use in a class presentation to the school entitled, 'Stand up for what you believe in'. As a class, agree how the presentation will be made; will it be a PowerPoint presentation, a display, a school assembly? Once the type of presentation is agreed, give each pair a time limit to prepare. Arrange for the presentation to the whole school.

Extension
Suggest the class research volunteer opportunities for children on the internet and through the local library.

Activity 12: My rights and responsibilities

Talk about what the children have learned about their rights and responsibilities in their communities during the unit. Suggest that the children draw a mind map with themselves in the middle of a sheet of paper, surrounded by each of their communities, with a record of their important rights and responsibilities for each community in its bubble. Make a display of these mind maps with a 'Rights and responsibilities of Year X' heading.

Display the **Rights and responsibilities** cards from the CD-ROM on the whiteboard. Organise the children into groups of four or six and ask half of the groups to choose a 'right' and the other half to choose a 'responsibility' card. Each group should then write arguments both for and against their right or responsibility. They should reach a 'conclusion' in their groups which they can relay to the class. The **Arguments** template will support them in this activity.

Look at 'Stories: What young people have achieved' on the UNICEF website www.unicef.org (via the CRC@18 section). Ask the children, in groups, to think about one of these young people. What do they think of the young person and their achievement? Do they think it was difficult? Do they think they could achieve something like this?

Give each child a copy of the **Reflection** template and ask them to complete it independently. They should then make up their cube, and add it to a display in the library, where others can think about these rights and responsibilities.

Children can now complete the self-evaluation sheet or the children's booklet for the unit.

Unit 6

My community and environment

Photocopiable: Activity 2 **C**

Needs and wants – a different perspective

Think about your needs and wants. Make a list of your five most important needs and wants, in order.

Needs	Wants
1. _____	_____
2. _____	_____
3. _____	_____
4. _____	_____
5. _____	_____

Now, pretend you live in a developing world country and answer these questions.

Where do you live? _____

List your four most important needs and wants, in order.

Needs	Wants
1. _____	_____
2. _____	_____
3. _____	_____
4. _____	_____

Are the needs the same? _____

Why would the needs and wants be different to your own?

_____

Photocopiable: Activity 3

Unit 6

My community and environment

Survey of facilities for disabled people

Venue for survey _____
Date _____

1. How many disabled car parking spaces are available?
a ☐ Two or more
b ☐ One
c ☐ None

2. Is there good access for disabled people, for example a ramp for wheelchair users, help for blind or deaf people?
a ☐ Yes
b ☐ Not directly, but with a detour or help provided
c ☐ No

3. How disabled-friendly is the reception area, for example can wheelchair users speak to receptionists; are there facilities for those with hearing or sight disabilities?
a ☐ Yes, communication is possible for those with varying disabilities
b ☐ There is some help with communication
c ☐ No, communication would be very difficult

4. Are all areas of the venue accessible for those with disabilities?
a ☐ Yes, there are lifts and ramps throughout the building and corridors are wide so no area is inaccessible
b ☐ Most areas are accessible, but some are not
c ☐ No, most areas are inaccessible

5. Does the venue have a hearing loop for deaf visitors?
a ☐ Yes, there is a hearing loop throughout the venue
b ☐ Some areas have a hearing loop
c ☐ No, there is no hearing loop

6. Is the signage through the building large and clear for those with sight disabilities?
a ☐ Yes, all the signs are large and clear
b ☐ Some of the signs are large and clear
c ☐ Only one or two signs fulfil these criteria

7. Are there disabled toilets?
a ☐ More than one and meet minimum requirements
b ☐ One only, and not accessible for all
c ☐ No

8. Is there any additional specific help for people with disabilities, for example signs in Braille, a person dedicated to helping those with disabilities?
a ☐ Yes there are a number of additional specific initiatives for disabled people
b ☐ There is talk of some additional initiatives being implemented
c ☐ No, and none are planned

How did the venue score?
Mostly a's: *The facilities for disabled people are excellent and they will feel welcome.*
Mostly b's: *There are some facilities for disabled people, but more could be done to make them feel welcome.*
Mostly c's: *There are poor facilities, and the venue should be doing more for disabled people.*

Unit 6

My community and environment

Cheating

Look at these illustrations. What would you do in each situation?

Do you think this is right?
_____

Why/why not?
_____

What would you do?
_____

Who could you tell?
_____

Go on, let me have a look at your project, no one will know!

Do you think this is right?
_____

Why/why not?
_____

What would you do?
_____

Who could you tell?
_____

Health & Wellbeing ages 9-11

Self-evaluation

Unit 6

My community and environment

My community and environment

Before you complete this sheet, think carefully about all of the activities you have done in this unit. Look at the displays in the classroom and check back on some of the work in your books and folders.

Make a list of the most important things that you have learned during this unit.

_____

_____

What do you know now that you didn't know before?

_____

What can you do now that you couldn't do before?

_____

What or who helped you to learn? Explain.

_____

What hindered your learning? Explain.

_____

How would you rate your effort and learning during this unit?

_____

What do you still need to learn about this topic?

_____

What questions would you still like to have explored and answered?

_____

_____

_____

_____

SCHOLASTIC

Also available in this series:

ISBN 978-1407-10020-3

ISBN 978-1407-10021-0

ISBN 978-1407-10022-7

ISBN 978-1407-10023-4

Also available for Scotland:

ISBN 978-1407-10024-1

ISBN 978-1407-10025-8

ISBN 978-1407-10026-5

ISBN 978-1407-10027-2

To find out more, call: 0845 603 9091
or visit our website www.scholastic.co.uk